Change Your Conversation, Change Your Life

JOHN MICHAEL HOOVER

"A gem. It's that simple … a gem.

"When given the opportunity to comment concerning my feelings about *Change Your Conversation,* those were my first thoughts. Whether referring to Lani, Malinda, or *Change Your Conversation,* simply "a gem" is all that needs to be said….but upon further thought I realized that doesn't explain waiting patiently each day for 'Think About It,' the daily inspirational quote from Lani and Malinda, or searching through archived e-mails for details of a past 'Think About It' whose premise suddenly returned to occupy my every thought.

"Nor does it explain my 'favorite,' which I have written on a card and keep in my wallet, even though I have it memorized and remove it from my wallet several times a day to read it aloud because I want to see it and hear it and speak it and act upon it and tell everyone within hearing distance about it. It's the one that has been known to lead to instantaneous -- *yes, I meant to say instantaneous* -- changes in your outlook, your life situation, and your immediate future.

"The ideas, thoughts, and spectacular new cutting-edge scientific concepts assembled here are doubtless destined to touch and change lives in the same, and even far greater, ways than they have changed mine. This is innovative, from the heart, and most importantly, information you can use now, today, no practice required!

"I have just come to the realization that I was correct with my first reaction.

"A gem, it's that simple … a gem."

GLENN MCNEMAR

"*Change Your Conversation, Change Your Life* is a revolutionary approach to teaching and living the wisdom we aspire to in every great ancient and contemporary spiritual tradition. Many years ago when I was physically a much younger man, I felt my innate happiness and connectedness. I intuitively felt my spirituality and knew I was part of something much bigger than myself. The people I surrounded myself with, and the activities I engaged in, made me feel good and capable of achieving anything. I had a positive outlook and a strong sense of well-being.

"Over the years, however, I unknowingly allowed negative energy into my life. The people I became entangled with challenged and eroded my positive belief system. I became distracted and lost sense of my true nature. My world was consumed with negativity and, for many years, I felt completely lost and disconnected from my true self.

"When I finally hit rock bottom, I began searching for answers. It was then I discovered the wonderful insight offered by *Change Your Conversation*. This intelligent and intuitive book distills the vast wisdom and collective knowledge of the greatest spiritual leaders and sages of the ages down to one simple, useable message -- we all engage in conversation, and that conversation can be used as a tool to convey the positive energy we desire to manifest in our lives. Everything in this universe is energy and we can use that energy to move our lives. The most important thing we can do after reading this book is to actively have these conversations with the person standing next to us so that more people are aware of our innate ability to be present, choose thoughts that serve us, and live happier lives."

Change Your Conversation, Change Your Life

MALINDA DOWSETT
& LANI BARNA

Change Your Conversation, Change Your Life
All Rights Reserved.
Copyright © 2011 Malinda Dowsett & Lani Barna
v3.0

ISBN PB: 978-0-578-08684-2
ISBN HB: 978-0-578-08700-9

Change Your Conversation Publications

Library of Congress Control Number: 2011931562

PRINTED IN THE UNITED STATES OF AMERICA

ACKNOWLEDGMENTS

Malinda

To Lani, incredible friend and business partner,
Thank you for walking into my life and showing me how to create a path of
love and compassion
for myself and all others.
Thank you for taking this incredible journey with me.
I wouldn't be here without you, girl.

To my parents,
Bill and Ann Carter,
for your love, presence, and never-ending support.
I love you.

To my Dad,
for encouraging and believing in me.

To my brothers,
David and Billy, for being here for me always.

To my amazing friends and family,
who lift me up in so many ways.
I love each and every one of you.

To my three beautiful children, Troy, Hailey, and Ty,
Thank you for choosing me.
You are my world and my true inspiration.
I love you as the powerful creators you are
and with all of my heart.

Last but not least, to Mark,
Without you, I would not have found me.

Malinda

Lani

Anyone who knows us knows this journey would never have been possible without Malinda,
who offers me the rarest of friendships
and the chance to express my true purpose under her watchful and guiding eye.
I love you, girl. Thank you for creating this beautiful thing with me.

To my mom,
who invited me to join her on the most important journey of her life.
I miss you.

And my dad,
without whom I would not be able to teach
what I know today.

To my treasured family and friends,
especially my beautiful daughter, Chessa,
I love each and every one of you.

Last, but not least,
To all the great wisdom teachers and spiritual masters who came before us, we would never be having these meaningful conversations without your great love, compassion, and desire to be in service to others.

Deepak Chopra, Mother Teresa, His Holiness the Dalai Lama, Wayne Dyer, Abraham, Esther and Jerry Hicks, Debbie Ford, Elizabeth Lesser, Robert Thurman, Timothy Freke, Fred Alan Wolf, Amit Goswami, Mike Dooley, Norman Vincent Peale, Edgar Cayce, Richard Carlson, Jack Canfield, Barbara De Angelis, Jack Kornfield, Michael Berg, Rhonda Bryne, Neale Donald Walsch, Stephen Hawking, Dale Noelting, Albert Einstein, Seth, Laurie Beth Jones, John Hagelin, Dean Radin, Lynne McTaggert, David Albert, Gregg Braden, Buddha, Barbara Marciniak, Rabindranath Tagore, Joe Dispenza, Sakyong Mipham, Pema Chondron, Michael Carroll, the Pleiadians, Ramtha, Fr. Anthony DeMello, Thomas Merton, Marianne Williamson, and my high school science teacher, Nelson Geiger, to name a few.

Lani

TABLE OF CONTENTS

FOREWORD

TWO WEEKS BEFORE THIS BOOK went to the publisher, I began hearing Malinda say, "Oh, I'm already past that," meaning this book. Before cover, jacket, or even one book in print, Malinda was on to the next book on relationships. She already knew this book was done, its message well-received and a basis established for another important area of our lives -- the relationships we choose to have with others in this lifetime. She knew that once you read this book and understood the potentiality and depth of the relationship you can have with yourself, everything else, beginning with the relationships around you, falls into place.

That's moving karma forward. You get to the point where the moment you see manifestation of what you want, you move forward again. Karma in play. Looking around, appreciating what you see, and moving on. Like you are riding the back of a giant and whispering in its ear.

Enjoy this book.
Discover your potentiality.
We did. You can too.

~ Lani and Malinda

INTRODUCTION

"What you talk about, you think about, and what you think about, you bring about. Every single time."

CHANGE YOUR CONVERSATION HAS STARTED a movement of understanding just how powerful you really are, and how you can learn to use that power to create a life that feels like the happiness, love, and joy we all seek. Happiness is nothing more than recognizing your own power, respecting it, embracing it, and taking total responsibility for the world you create around you.

Using quantum physics and neurobiology to weave a rich, new understanding of our spirituality, creators Malinda Dowsett and Lani Barna share how they overcame divorce, suicide, near death, single parenthood, huge financial loss, self-doubt, and negative internal chatter by changing their conversation. They show us how to recognize counterproductive thinking in casual conversation, misplaced expectations, and when we are painfully holding on to an idea that does not exist. They show us how to listen in on our internal conversations so we can re-shape them and use them as tools to continually, and graciously, move and expand our lives, always toward what feels better.

Change Your Conversation is about creating a new mind map to harness the power and energy behind every thought we have. It is about using our conversations to focus our attention -- and intention -- at the same time. That's power, because every conversation we have forecasts what we are allowing, and asking, to come our way.

*"Our mission is to touch a million lives,
and for that million to turn around and touch a million more
so we are all creating a karmic wave of changing conversations
together."*

Change Your Conversation is founded on four basic understandings that apply to each and every event and circumstance of your life: Thoughts, Feelings, Inner Guidance, and Choice – the "how" of the law of attraction. Using personal experience, Malinda and Lani demonstrate how to shift your attention and change the energy vibration you hold yourself to. Every time you change your vibration, you set yourself up to receive a very different kind of experience into your life.

This book you are reading is living proof that everything begins with a thought, and every thought has the potential to grow into an idea, and every idea can become so real that you can touch it, see it, feel it, and hear it around you. You are touching and feeling an idea that began in Malinda's kitchen one evening when we realized we were changing our lives. *Change Your Conversation* is the very first step to every new thing you want to see in your life because if you can't talk about what you want, you don't know what you want. You have to be able to talk about what you want down to the finest, finest detail, to have what you want around you. Everything you want begins with YOU.

Malinda's Story. After being married for six years, separated for a year, and then losing my husband to suicide in 2005, my life was in complete shambles. On the outside everybody thought I was doing pretty well until I decided to remarry a year later out of complete fear. At that point in my life I had never been so scared. I was raising two children on my own, running my own business, and totally separated from myself. All my life I thought I was supposed to be married, work hard, be a good mom and a loving person, and the rest would come out in the wash. When my husband died, I wasn't sure what direction I was moving in anymore. I felt lost and completely alone.

My conversations with myself were ones of despair, guilt, depression, and anger. I didn't think I had it in me to stand on my own two feet – as a matter of fact, I didn't want to stand on my own two feet. Deep down I didn't think I was capable of taking care of myself, much less my children. I woke up every morning wanting someone to just take it all away. I didn't have the strength to deal with the enormous pain I was carrying around. I thought if I just kept going, all of it would eventually go away.

Two years into a second marriage, I was emotionally and mentally at absolute rock bottom. I had totally isolated myself from my family and friends; my second marriage was incredibly unhealthy; and every thought I had about me, my life, and what I had become beat me up and tore me down. My life felt angry, depressed, anxious, guilty, and meaningless. Whatever deeply ingrained emotional issues were driving my life reflected pain back to me. I knew I was destined to continue this pattern of self-destruction if something didn't change. It was like waking up each day and rearranging deck chairs on the Titanic knowing that the end result would keep repeating itself as a complete disaster. Unless I wanted more of the same, I was going to have change from the inside out, but where to begin? That was the day I received an e-mail from an old friend, Lani Barna.

Lani and I had not spoken for two years, and her e-mail was a wake-up call. We very quickly picked up right where we left off, spending long hours on the phone talking about what had come our way and where we were in our respective lives. Our conversations had always been more on the spiritual side, and during the two years we had been apart, Lani had been on a journey of self-discovery.

She spent two years alone working through deeply troubling issues of loss: divorce, a highly valued job, and friends attached to that job. With great intent born of debilitating self-loathing and an overwhelming sense of despair, she turned away from external things and began studying everything she could get her hands on about being human. Who am I? Where am I going, what is going on around me, and what am I supposed to do while I am here?

> Self-knowledge is key to a healthy
> relationship with ourselves
> and others.
> His Holiness, the Dalai Lama
> ⌒◦⌒

She examined every belief she had about herself and others. She was intrigued by the idea that thoughts become things and turned to quantum physics to know why, neurobiology to know how, and her imagination and dreams to uncover purpose. She found that the only thing we ever need to do to have the life we want is to practice the life we want. So we started practicing together. We started, consciously and intentionally, to practice our dreams.

Every dream will begin to unfold the minute you stop asking the question, "Why is this happening _to_ me?" and begin asking, "Why is this happening _for_ me?" because each of these questions feels very different. The first question takes us down the path of victimhood, martyrdom, and feeling like we are never good enough or like something is wrong with us. The second question gives meaning to our lives, awakens self-knowledge, and allows us to heal.

Every conversation we have does much more than act as a medium for expressing thoughts and feelings. The language we use to express ourselves creates and shapes our thoughts and feelings as well.

Whether we were standing in the kitchen or talking on the phone, every conversation we had became a journey of moving our attention past where we were at the beginning of the conversation, and towards what we wanted by the time we said goodbye. We looked at old stories that no longer felt good and used them to verbalize how we really wanted to feel. We stepped back and looked at experiences that no longer served us and reflected on them: Is this really what I believe a marriage should feel like? Is this really the example I want to be giving my kids? Is this really how I want to feel about my job?

We stopped pushing others to change their ways to make us happy. We examined every painful story we told, searching for carefully hidden, well-crafted, misplaced expectations. We realized that with every misplaced expectation, we had caused many more to form, until the pain was unbearable. One by one we took back bits of ourselves we had unknowingly given away, and one by one we decided how we wanted to feel. We began to discover who we were and what we were made of. Am I courageous? Am I kind? Do I think it is possible to be happy -- and, if not, why not?

As we began to uncover and express our core beliefs -- is this really who I think I am? Is this really what I want to be? -- we realized the ground floor of every conversation either builds us up or tears us down. We began to look for the trigger thought at the beginning of every story we told – does this opening line make me feel good? Does this story, even before it is being told, feel bad? Then we began to choose. We began to choose happy.

As I became increasingly aware of my thoughts and how they made me feel, as I began to become aware of my Inner Guidance speaking to me, and my capacity to choose, I began seeing more and more opportunity to move my life in the direction I really wanted to go. I started to feel like I was taking back control of my life. I began to rediscover long-forgotten strengths. I began building myself back up a little bit more every day, and creating a better-feeling life, one conversation at a time.

I separated from my second husband four short months after Lani walked back into my life and showed me to myself again. With new eyes and an open mind, I let go of the past by finding gratitude for what I had learned and what life had caused me to become. I chose a new path based on the very foundation of my most treasured core belief – creating a loving home for myself and my children. I became incredibly quiet after allowing the drama of other people to be my concern no longer. I relaxed after breaking through all the major issues in my life. I found enormous strength from every event in my life that had once upon a time caused me pain. I discovered freedom from releasing old beliefs and ideas that no longer served me, and reveled in the space that opened up around me for the things I truly believe in and enjoy. Today, I am no longer in limbo. Today, I am living my dream. I openly and loudly and clearly choose a life that feels like love, joy, and happiness to me -- and I do it every day through my conversations.

In January 2010 Lani and I took a leap of faith and began sharing our story with the world. We put our toes in the water and began speaking to groups of people, ranging from women suffering domestic abuse and violence, to corporate executives, businesswomen, community leaders, and friends. No matter what the venue or who the audience, we talk about real ways to use every conversation we have to uncover fear and speak our core beliefs. We call it the power of conversation -- and *Change Your Conversation* was born.

Join us now on a journey of real self-discovery. Learn the science behind being human – learn who you are. Understand that your thoughts are like a magnet, and to think is to create.

"Life isn't about finding yourself. Life is about creating yourself." ~ George Bernard Shaw

We challenge you to start living the life you want today. Tell us what you want and we will tell you what you can have. Everything in your life positively begins and ends with YOU.

CHAPTER ONE
WHO YOU REALLY ARE

Your purpose isn't a mystery. It is to grow as a conscious human being, discover your gifts, accept your power, shed disempowering relationships, build a network of loving support and make a genuine contribution to humanity. Your purpose – and message – is your life lived.

WE ALL HAVE A STORY. Some of us tell the same story over and over again, and some of us continually evolve our story of what is to come. These stories, crafted over many years, make up every conversation we have.

Changing your conversation is the fastest and most effective way to create the life you want, because every story you tell about your life is the law of attraction at work. Deliberately changing your conversation – the way you talk about your life – from the big, big things to the little, little things -- changes the vibration you hold yourself to and every experience you attract into your life. Change your conversation, change your vibration, and you change your life.

It begins by knowing who you are.

All of us have heard of the law of attraction throughout our lives. This concept, we assure you, is nothing new. All the great wisdom traditions speak of it. Here are a few of the ways you describe it:

"What goes around comes around."
"Birds of a feather flock together."
"What you put out you get back."
"What you sow you shall reap."
"Misery loves company."
"Do unto others as you would have them do unto you."

The law of attraction is a fundamental nature of reality. It is observable and predictable and, as you can see from the quotes above, we actually talk about it all the time. You can very quickly tell how the law of attraction is working in your life by listening in on the conversations you have with yourself and others. Notice the words you use. Visualize the ideas you share. How do they feel? Your conversations are physical manifestation of the thoughts you allow your attention to rest on. And the vibration you hold yourself to is how those thoughts make you feel.

Conversations that are full of angry, jealous, indignant, righteous, or hurtful thoughts have a distinct feeling -- they feel heavy and burdensome: a low, dull vibration. Conversations filled with inspired, loving, grateful, kind, and compassionate thoughts feel lighter: they have an expansive feeling, a higher vibration. The way your conversations make you feel is an authentic indicator of what you are creating, and allowing, to flow your way.

Your attention (what you think about) and your intention (what you believe) are what bring the law of attraction to life. But before you can understand how it works, you have to know who you are. To truly understand how we create our lives, we need to go back to school and take a look at four parts of us we cannot see.

Thoughts
Where do they come from? What do they do?

Feelings
Every thought has a feeling.

Inner Guidance
The other person you talk to when no one else is in the room.

Choice
How to know which choice best serves you.

Thoughts, Feelings, Inner Guidance, and Choice are the ground floor of every decision, event, experience, situation, circumstance, and person in your life. They are an internal framework so subtle that unless given good information, we cannot possibly know they exist.

Thoughts, Feelings, Inner Guidance, and Choice are the innate potential that lies dormant within each of us to manage thought. They are a subprogram, so to speak, in the background of your mind that connects you with you. They are how the law of attraction works -- how to move any aspect of your life past what is and towards where you want it to be.

Every time you are able to step back and observe your thoughts, every time you pause, look at, and decide to direct your thoughts, you are in control of that aspect of your life. Every time you choose because of you, you build you up, and when you build you up, that feeling feels SO GOOD that you will never, ever give away that feeling – the feeling of YOU -- again. Rumi calls it "a river of joy."

YOU, who is underneath all the drama and major issues in your life. YOU, who is underneath the old beliefs and mistaken ideas that you have about yourself and others. YOU, who is a treasure of enormous strength and gratitude for all the life experiences that once caused you pain. YOU, who can open up a huge amount of space in your life for the things you truly want and believe in. This is the beginning of every path of true peace, joy, and happiness -- self-knowledge – knowing who YOU really are.

You are physical and non-physical at the same time.

Science tells us something very different today about what it means to be human. There is more to us than we have been led to believe. It is time to openly talk about the huge disparity between how we appear and how we really are.

Quantum physics tells us that all matter -- you, me, everything -- exists on two planes simultaneously. We are physical and non-physical at the same time. The physical plane is everything we perceive with our five senses: hearing, taste, touch, smell and sight. The non-physical is a field of energy and the basic building block of everything we observe and call physical. EVERYTHING is energy.

This non-physical side of you has been called many things throughout the ages:

Spirit
Conscience
Consciousness
Soul
Intuition
Aura
Chakra
Karma
Inner Wisdom
Inner Guide

Each of these words is talking about the same thing – intelligent energy, pure positive energy, the non-physical side of you.

Did you know that every cell in your body emits 1.14 volts of electricity? Multiply that by *52 trillion cells,* and you can easily see we are walking, talking, energy beings and our thoughts are how we focus our non-physical energy – the power behind our thoughts -- into the physical world.

Think of a thought as a magnifying glass, or an interface between the seen and unseen. Quantum physics tells us that whatever we give our attention to, whatever we observe, whatever we focus on snaps into existence and becomes our reality, or experience. It is called the Copenhagen interpretation, or collapse of the wave function -- the concept that everything in the subatomic world exists as a probability, and that measurement (our attention) plays an ineradicable role (http://en.wikipedia.org/wiki/Copenhagen_interpretation).

What this means is that there is a dynamic connection between our thoughts and life around us, which is always in play. It doesn't matter whether we are thinking negative thoughts or positive thoughts, limiting thoughts or unlimited thoughts, degrading thoughts or uplifting thoughts; we are always crafting our world around us. Our attention is what brings thought to life.

Think of the non-physical you as part of an immense field of energy, which everything rises from. Not only do we arise from it, but we are directly connected to it. This field of energy is like a huge copying machine and your thoughts are the switch. The more intense a thought, the more energy you put into the field to connect with. No matter what you think about – from the big, big things to the little, little things – what you are always thinking about will manifest over time. What we think about always becomes our reality. Becoming aware of what you think about is the first step in knowing why you function as you do.

This energy -- "all that is" -- is expressed as particles in our physical world, which is really what quantum physics is all about. "Quantum" means "small" and "physics" means "the nature of." Quantum physics is the study of really small things that make up the field of energy that is in us and around us. We tap into this energy all the time.

Every time you lift your face to the sun, you feel the energy of photons warming your face. Every time you smell perfume, it is molecular activity that you cannot see. Plug in a toaster and electrons we call electricity are at your disposal. Scan your groceries or change a channel, and the electromagnetic radiation we call wireless is used. Even NASA is using particle physics to ramp up space travel for warp speed. A new propulsion engine is being developed using the energy of super-heated particles we call plasma, more commonly known as our sun (http://www.classroomclips.org/video/1503).

We are always tapped into this field of energy. We are always affecting each other and everything around us on a subatomic scale. Our electrons are always doing a little back-and-forth dance of energy and exchanging information with everything around us. When you hear the idea that we are all connected, we are. Everything we do affects the field.

Taking back your power begins here. Look around your life without judgment, understanding that you totally and completely created it all with the energy of the thoughts you were thinking at the time. Take responsibility, own it, embrace it, and evolve with it. So whether you created good things or bad things, know they are the result of past thinking. You are always at the edge of your creation. You have the power within you to change direction at any time, with one thought, and start anew. Just as you have taught yourself to behave, react, or be the way you are today because of how you chose to look at the circumstances and experiences in your life at one time, you have the ability to behave, react, or be different by changing the way you choose to look at those same circumstances and experiences today.

When you decide to take full responsibility for your life, you will be one of the few. Everywhere you turn, you bump up against patterned thinking of the masses because for many, it is easier to believe that their lives just happen -- that they are the result, not the cause. Powerlessness is in every newspaper, every television show, and in almost every conversation you overhear. If you want to break the bonds of limiting beliefs -- that you aren't good enough, smart enough, thin enough, or right enough -- you must give yourself permission to believe that it is possible for you to have creative control over your life. You must give yourself permission to explore the possibility of designing a life that works for you.

There are those who believe that "what goes around, comes around" refers only to physical actions. If I do the right thing, everything will happen as it is supposed to. But right and wrong does not go far enough. How many married couples remain in an unhappy day-to-day existence because they are supposed to? Right action is only half of the equation. Nature is duality – physical and non-physical. Every thought, word, and deed we express either evolves us or regresses us. So while doing good deeds is most definitely a good thing, the energy behind our thoughts -- our intention – which is always expressed through our conversation, has an even greater effect on the energy field around us.

Conversations filled with pain, blame, guilt, anger, anxiety, depression, or justification affect the space you and everybody around you is in. Everybody feels the energy of what you bring into your space. If you feel inspired, they feel inspired. If you feel sad, they feel sad.

How about when you are always harping on every negative thing that ever happens to you? The more you harp, the worse your life feels; and the worse your life feels, the more you harp. You must understand that this vicious cycle is you practicing telling a painful story over and over and over again.

How about the conversations you have with yourself? Do you find yourself spinning out of control, or on a downward spiral that relives, and exaggerates, painful memories even though what you are remembering has absolutely nothing to do with what is going on right here, right now? This is how we practice getting lost in our mind.

Learning to break vicious cycles of thinking may seem difficult at first. It may feel as if a ping-pong game is going on inside your head, and for a while, there will be. Just like everything else in life, taking control of your thoughts is a process that takes practice, and certainly takes time. This is where conversation comes in. You can see your thoughts every time you speak. You can monitor your thoughts all the time.

So the first step is easy. Want to know what you practice in your mind every day? Listen to the stories you tell. If your stories feel great, congratulate yourself! You need to change nothing. However, if the stories you tell feel like pain, guilt, depression, anger, or fear, the second step of taking control is to replace them with ones that feel better. We call this "creating a new mind map." If you don't give the brain a new direction to follow, it will pick up right where it left off. It will continue to think, do, and be the way it has always been. Here's why:

According to neuroscience the brain is aware only of what is familiar. It is capable of processing only information that reinforces past experiences of your life. Every event, circumstance, impression, feeling, person, and place we have ever experienced is hard wired into the brain. Every

> Until you dream,
> there isn't a map.
> Until you speak, you don't know.
> Until you move, there isn't a path.
> Everything you want in life
> positively begins with, ends with,
> and is about you.
>
> 〜∂〜

time we have a new experience, our brain only allows information in that reinforces what it already knows. Our environment causes us to think. Like a computer program, it mindlessly re-creates life as you know it until you give it something new to see.

We know that less than one billionth of the stimuli available to us in any given moment makes it into our nervous system. We also know that the brain processes over 400,000 bits of information a second, but allows us to be aware of only 2000 of those bits. What this tells us is that we miss a whole lot of what is going on.

We also have the ability to turn our attention away from thoughts all the time, whether we know it or not. As you concentrate on this book, perhaps you have forgotten about the argument you had with your boss this morning, or the overdraft notice in the mail when you got home, or even what gender you are.

In *Evolve Your Brain*, Joe Dispenza makes the point that if the only information our brain is capable of allowing into our awareness is information equal to its environment, and if we never think outside the box, if we never think of the possibilities in our lives, if we never think beyond "what is," what do we get? More of "what is," over and over and over again. To truly change, then, is to think and act greater than our environment. To do this requires new knowledge and repetition. New knowledge includes dreams and possibilities that introduce new information into the brain and force the brain to work in new ways. New information is the catalyst that causes the brain to form new circuits and make new connections. New circuits and new connections are how we build a new mind map to give the brain, and ourselves, a new direction to go.

The only question is: how long can you hold onto a new thought, a better-feeling thought? How long are you willing to give your brain to integrate new information into what it already knows?

Real change takes practice. Real change takes a conscious act of will.

Is it really possible to completely change the way we react and behave? Studies show that as long as we are alive and breathing, we have the ability to change our mind. Neuroplasticity is the brain's ability to change based on experience (http://en.wikipedia.org/wiki/Neuroplasticity). The brain is capable of building a new mind map every time we can visualize an expanded version of our lives. Dreams are how we visualize expanded versions of our lives.

Let's go back to the subatomic world for a moment. Most people think of particles – electrons – that make up you as little billiard balls bouncing around all over the place. But particles are not matter; they are more like a wave of possibilities until they are measured, or observed. What this means to you is that in any given moment there are an endless number of possibilities for you to choose from.

Think about it. At this very moment, you could pick up a pen and start writing, you could get up and get something to eat, you could put this book down and turn on the TV, stand up, scratch your ear, daydream about tomorrow, or cross your legs. Whichever thought you choose to focus on collapses all possibilities into one, and your choice becomes real to YOU. This is why thoughts become things. When you observe a thought, when you focus on a thought, it ceases to be one of many in a vast wave of possibilities and takes on form that we can perceive.

On the flip side, when you stop giving your attention to a thought, your brain stops firing neurons associated with that thought and old connections – old mind maps – wither and die. Think back to a time in your life when you were consumed with puppy love in high school for someone you were sure you couldn't live without. You couldn't eat, you couldn't sleep. You thought about this love of your life twenty-four hours a day.

Do you think of that person today? They are no longer in your everyday awareness, are they? This is because neurons that fire together, wire together. Neurons that stop firing wither and die. We experience reality because we give our attention to it. We also experience reality based on how we feel.

In his brilliant book, *Evolve Your Brain,* Dispenza recounts two simple experiments that clearly demonstrate how we interpret the world.

At the University of Pennsylvania studies were done to show that people see the world equal to how they feel. If you take a group of people who are depressed and a group of people who are emotionally happy and show both groups of people an equal number of slides of wedding pictures and funeral pictures, guess which slides the depressed people say they saw more of? Funeral pictures.

And the group that was emotionally happy? Wedding pictures.

We perceive reality based on the way we feel, which means just because we have a thought doesn't mean it is true.

In another experiment a group of volunteers were asked to wear prism glasses for two weeks, which turned everything they looked at upside down. They were asked to wear these glasses all the time -- when they took their children to school, when they cooked dinner, when they went to bed. Despite great discomfort, the volunteers wore them and at the end of two weeks, when they returned to the lab, they were asked to describe what they saw. Every person said the same thing: "I see fine."

No, no, no, they were told. You have prism glasses on, you should be seeing everything upside down. No, they responded, we see everything just fine.

Just because we have a thought doesn't mean it's true.

These were some of the first experiments in neuroscience that told us that the brain sees, not the eyes, because if the eyes see, they would see everything upside down, and they would see the correct number of slides. Your brain overlays reality based on memory. Your brain fills in the picture of the external world based on the way you perceive the past. Your brain will keep you exactly where you are, because that's all it knows.

How many times have you proofread a paper and missed typos because your brain expects to see the correct word? How many times have you misunderstood a situation because you remember what has happened to you in the past? "She didn't answer my e-mail last week. She is so rude! He didn't say anything about the information I sent him. He must hate it." So many times we "see" what is going on right here, right now, through the eyes of memory.

> We suffer when we allow ourselves to hold on to an idea that does not exist.
> Be present: right here, right now.
> Look around you -- you are just fine. Consult with the greater part of you and allow your inner self to guide you along your path. You are meant to be a strong, vibrant, independent, and courageous creator. Let go of ideas that no longer serve you, and MOVE.
>
> ⌒✿⌒

Every experience is neutral until you give it meaning. In other words, the only meaning anything ever has is that which you give it. Our perception labels an experience happy or sad, good or bad, positive or negative in accordance with what we believe about ourselves, which is also part of our perception.

This is why all of us see the world completely different and all of us can change what we see. This is why there are as many realities as there are perceivers. The next time you find yourself arguing with your spouse, family, or co-worker, frustrated because they can't seem to get it right, irritated because they just don't understand, YOU understand that there is no reality out there. Everybody sees their world based on past experience, and no two experiences or realities are alike. Stephen Hawking calls it "model dependent reality." Reality is structured and assembled in the brain. It isn't that difficult people aren't doing things right, it's that you expect them to do things the way you have it structured in YOUR brain. You expect them to perform the way you do. You expect them to do, say, or be the way you would do, say, or be.

This is the foundation of all misplaced expectations. This is how we cause ourselves to needlessly suffer.

You are not here to change anything. You are here to realize and awaken the potential of you. Just as we no longer believe that the sun rises in the east and sets in the west, just as we no longer believe that the world is flat, you no longer need to believe that the world consists of external events, people, and circumstances that you have to control. You no longer need to feel small, powerless, or at the mercy of others' moods and actions.

Everything you "see" is built in your mind through beliefs and ideas you have collected over the years. The people, places, and things in your life are your reality. They are all specific to your neuronet, which you built with every tiny decision and every unformed choice you made along the way. They are specific to the reality you are currently in. To change your reality, you have to change an idea you have about the people, places, things, or events of your life. When you understand this, everything – and we mean EVERYTHING -- changes.

You are the reality you are creating. It bears saying then, that there is power in being present in your life. When you can stand in the middle of it and look around it with love, there is power when every moment feels timeless and three-dimensional because every molecule in it belongs to you.

This is the fundamental nature of reality: how you feel. How you feel is everything, because when you can feel what you want around you, what you want is here.

CHAPTER TWO
LET YOUR FEELINGS GUIDE YOU

How do you consciously create your life?
Practice verbalizing a story that feels better, a story that serves you better.
Begin taking charge of every conversation in and around you.
Clearly, kindly, compassionately say, "I choose what I allow into my life."

TO CONNECT WITH THE GREATER part of you -- your inner self -- you have to be aware of how thoughts make you feel all the time.

> Every conversation we have says: this is who I am, this is what I am, this is why I am. Some of us do not see a way out of the economic crisis we are in today. This is who I am: I am afraid. Some of us study our own mind. This is what I am: I am more than this physical body. Some of us are constantly recreating and evolving our patterns of thought and behavior. This is why I am: I am alive.
>
> ༒

Every thought has a very direct feeling. Many of us teach ourselves to disconnect, disengage, and react our way through life based on previous experience. But have you listened to yourself along the way? Stop making choices based on reaction and start making them based on what you truly want from the experience and how you want to feel about that part of your life. Otherwise, why are you in it? Teach yourself to connect and engage with what is really going on in every moment, and then respond. Respond based on how you want to feel when the experience is over. Respond based on how you want to feel twenty years from now. This is how you finesse your life.

Your feelings will guide you effortlessly. They are a direct connect with the non-physical you. Notice how you feel and you can immediately match the feeling with the thought that brought the feeling to you. This is how to become aware of which thoughts make you feel like you do. To do this, you have to get quiet and pause so a little bit of space opens up around you. That's how you tune in. You will never be able to choose something different if you can't focus long enough to know what you are really thinking and how those thoughts make you feel.

For some, getting quiet is a scary place to be. When you quiet your mind, you are going to immediately notice how you feel. For those of us still carrying around unresolved old hurts and unsatisfied desires, those feelings are going to resemble pain, anger, embarrassment, jealousy, or shame. This is where you practice trusting your feelings no matter what they are. They are all telling you something. Stop judging them. They have been given to you as a guide. Every time you know how you don't want to feel, you know exactly how you do want to feel. Stop resisting whatever it is you are feeling and just look at it so you can choose differently.

The Asking. "I need help in processing this HUGE anger I have for my ex-boyfriend. His abandonment of me over Christmas triggered some HUGE anger that is consuming my thoughts. I'm angry, hurt, and thinking toxic thoughts. I want a healthy relationship but I'm scared of starting over. I don't want this lonely feeling anymore. I have a tendency to isolate which exacerbates the problem and I seem to implode. So here's the pattern: I isolate, I get more toxic in my thinking, I gain weight (which has already started, I've put on seven pounds), and then I get depressed. I want someone to do life with, someone I can travel and have adventures with. I want to be with someone who wants to be with me. I want to feel important to someone.

"What I want is to be with someone whose eyes light up when he sees me, someone who calls me when there's a huge storm, someone who thinks about me driving my Smartcar in inclement weather, someone who values me. I want to be important to just one person. I feel very insignificant. No kids, no husband, no career. I feel like I don't fit in anywhere. I'm between twelve and twenty years younger than my siblings, so I never fit with them and I work somewhere that I really don't fit in because of the huge socio-economic differences in our lives. I run with a group of girls who have more money and freedom than I do and I don't fit with them either. I feel like I don't belong anywhere and I want to belong so badly. I want a family and it's looking like that isn't ever going to happen for me. I'm incredibly sad and lonely right now."

Malinda's Response. "I'm sorry to hear about your break-up and understand how difficult this is. Rest assured I will help you process through, because I have most definitely been there!

"So here's the deal, we have to shift your thinking. What you think about, you bring about. In order for you to move on and find the relationship of your dreams, you have to deal with what is at hand.

"This seems to be a cycle that keeps repeating itself over and over in all your relationships. You are focused on past events, what has happened in the past, what the reactions have been in the past -- and so you are recreating the past. We need to bring your thoughts to right here, right now.

"You said you feel as though you don't fit in anywhere. Understand that this is due to how you are choosing to look at each scenario. You are judging yourself. You perceive yourself as not fitting in. If your girl-friends didn't think you fit in, they wouldn't be your girlfriends. This is you beating yourself up. Don't believe every thought you have. You said you don't fit in with your siblings. Have they ever expressed that to you, or is this how you are choosing to look at the experiences? Perhaps this is a pattern of thinking you developed as a child because of the situation with your parents and being the youngest. Understand that just because your parents did not do for you what they did for the other children in your family does not mean that they loved you less... it means that they had their own issues to contend with and that has absolutely nothing to do with you.

"You say that you don't fit in anywhere, and I have to disagree with that. You are choosing to see yourself as not fitting in anywhere, and because you continue to look at those same experiences over and over with deeper conviction every time, then you are continually putting the law of attraction to work and bringing situations to you that do not feel good. So here goes ...

"As far as your ex-boyfriend goes, you are angry because your expectations are misplaced. You are expecting him to react, say, or do things the way you expect him to, on some level. You are expecting him to love and care for you the way that you want him to love and care for you, while at the same time you are doubting yourself, beating yourself up, and feeling insecure, which comes out in the relationship.

"In order for all of this to change and to bring about that which you really want, you have to start REALLY paying attention to every conversation that you are having with yourself. Stop allowing yourself to beat you up. Take a step back from all of the experiences that are holding you back and find the gift that has been given to you and only you. This is another chance for you to go back and look at the core of your being -- your childhood -- and find the gifts for you!

"You can start by seeing how strong and courageous you are. How beautiful you are from the inside out. How independent and smart you are. How savvy you are. All of these things come from your childhood, your upbringing, your parents. Once you can find the gifts, you can be grateful and then you can let it GO!

"When you start listening to the conversations that you are having, they very quickly tell you exactly what vibration you are holding yourself to. So, if you are always telling the stories of how awful your life is, how broke you are, or how mistreated you have been, then you are holding yourself to a very low, negative vibration. You feel horrible, powerless, helpless, and out of control. And if you are holding yourself to a negative vibration, and if like attracts like, then this is what you are getting...more of what you don't want.

"However, if you tune in and start changing your conversations from ones of anger, frustration, helplessness, powerless, and lack of control to ones of gratitude, forgiveness, and compassion -- immediately you feel your energy shift. Immediately you feel better. Immediately you feel a sense of relief. Immediately you have changed the vibration that you are holding yourself to, and are changing that which you are attracting into your world.

"So how does that apply to you? Begin journaling your thoughts, then go back and replace every thought with one that feels better to you. Now that you know what you don't want, what do you want? Keep replacing the old thoughts with new ones and very quickly you will begin to see where you are feeling better, you are seeing things in a different light, you will begin to see where you are beginning to move yourself in the right direction. This takes practice, practice, practice and you have to make a commitment to yourself to continually go back and look at your thought process ... is this what I truly believe? Is this what I want to bring into my reality? Is this what I want to attract into my life? Let go of the judging, defending, justifying, and blaming ... .they only hold you where you are!"

Whatever you are feeling, ask yourself, where is this coming from?

What purpose does it serve, and is it possible to feel differently? If not, why? Examine your pain. Roll it around and look at it. Look at it as if it belonged to someone else. Ask yourself, if I had a magic wand, what would I choose? What would I choose differently? Becoming familiar with your thoughts is how you fully participate in your life.

Every strong emotion comes from either love or fear. The next time you feel bad, whether you call it jealousy, hatred, victimization, depression, or unworthiness, ask yourself, *What am I afraid of?* Where is this coming from? Rather than being afraid of the answer, find the answer. Only then can you use it to shift your attention to how you really want to feel.

This is a process to live by. A healthy relationship with ourselves and others only happens when we give ourselves permission to examine and re-examine our lives. Every great Oscar-winning movie you have ever seen had tension in it. Tension is what causes the hero or heroine of the story to rise above, overcome, and grow. The same goes for you. Tension causes you to dig deep, find hidden strengths, gain wisdom, feel compassion, and grow. People who are afraid of emotion ignore how their conversations make them feel, which then intensify into conversations filled with the very emotion they find hard to control.

So feel your way through your life; don't roller-coaster your way through it. Emotions are nothing more than intensified feelings. Paying attention to how you are always feeling -- from the big, big things to the little, little things -- causes you to respond, not react habitually out of memory. If you are feeling uncomfortable in a situation, if little red flags are going off in your head, pay attention before the experience escalates in a direction you do not want to go. Relax and listen to your feelings. They are meant to guide you. They are designed to assist you on your journey, like breadcrumbs along the trail. Subtle clues which, when you allow them to, will lead you to the joy and happiness you seek. Fear is the only thing that stops us or holds us back from doing the things we want out of life. Fear of failing ourselves, fear of not succeeding, fear of doing something new, fear of what others will say.

Lani's Story. "While having dinner with a girlfriend, we began talking about relationships. 'Why are they so difficult?' she asked.

"Because it's never the person. It's always the feeling. Whenever you dream about the kind of relationship you want with a man, a woman, a sister, a mother, it always feels a certain way ... it resonates with you.

"So step back. Look at how the relationship you have feels today -- not two weeks ago or when you first started hanging out. Does it feel good? Is what you are feeling the way you want to feel?

"If the answer is no, then be kind to yourself, and be clear. Describe to yourself how you want this relationship to feel. Honor what you see. Be grateful. Understand how this current experience has helped you become even more clear about what you really want. Respect your inner voice -- your inner self, that part of you that always feels the same and never changes -- speaking to you in the only language it knows: feeling.

"Take time to get quiet. Sit down and write down all the words that come to mind when you think of the energy between you. Now go back and write down how each word makes you feel. Then choose what you want to feel.

"Begin by verbalizing who you are. This feels good to me. This does not feel good to me. Be clear. Be kind. Be in love with yourself. If you can't love yourself enough to verbalize what truly makes you happy, you can't have it --and the other people in your life will never know what resonates inside you either.

"It's never the person. It's always the feeling you are wanting to enjoy."

> When one door closes, many more open. So many times we want to continue looking at the closed door standing behind us, yet if we simply turn around and look up there's a field of opportunities holding the possibilities that we have been searching for. Everything in life unfolds just as it should: have faith, and trust that the universe has once again aligned you with all that you have been asking for. Relax, create, and inspire!
>
> ✐

When we operate out of fear, we regress our lives. We close the door on a better experience. We deny the fundamental reason for our existence, which is to become more than who we are. We miss out on opportunities to go back to the drawing board and create, yet again, a wiser, stronger you. We miss out on the chance to take our lives in a whole new direction. We miss out on our powerful ability to change.

We share Mike Dooley's keen observation that when you are feeling your lowest, the real you is summoned to appear. It is during these times that you heighten your awareness of how amazing you are because vulnerable doesn't mean powerless, scared doesn't mean lacking, and uncertainty doesn't mean that you're lost. It means you are in the process of becoming an extraordinary creation of you.

Tuning in to how you feel in every experience, in every moment, and in every conversation is a powerful guide. Feel your words. If your words feel fearful, you feel fear. If your words are open and generous, you feel expansive. If your words are inspired, you are inspiring others. Feel the world you are in. This is what it is all about. You are so much more than physical. You are pure energy, as is everything else. You are always pulling the energy of your thoughts, expressed by your words and the intention behind these words, toward you. You are always saying to the world, 'This is how I structure my reality. This is how I feel about my life.'

'Sometimes, it's hard to tell where other people end and the rest of your life begins. But there is a way to end this blur of identities, wants and needs. Pay attention to your natural feelings first. Pay attention to YOU first. Love yourself first. Be kind to yourself first. Only then can you love and be kind to others because you cannot, and will never, give away what you do not have.

> The universe does not know if the vibration you are offering is because of what you are imagining or what you are observing. In either case, it is responding. emotion is your guidance or response to your vibration. Your emotion does not create; it is an indicator of what you are already creating. ~ Abraham

We know there is no way to possibly keep track of every single thought that crosses your mind throughout the day. But you can tune in at any moment to how you feel. Make it a priority to feel, then think, your way through your day. Notice when you do not feel good. What are you thinking about? Notice when you are feeling angry or upset. What are you thinking about? Connect the feeling with the thought that brought it; otherwise, if left unchecked, you will find yourself on a downward spiral that you did not even realize was there. Every time you connect how you feel with the thought that feels that way, you can very quickly change the way you feel. Be vigilant as you practice listening to how you feel: this is how to shift your mind the moment you recognize you are feeling 'off.'

Some of you may be asking, 'Okay, I don't feel good. How do I shift my thoughts? I know these thoughts do not feel good. How do I break an awful downward spiral that I feel myself going on?'

Stop. Stop what you are doing and re-focus on what is going on here and now. Every time you find yourself going for a ride in your mind, lost in some ridiculous conversation with yourself about how horrible your life is or how your spouse isn't meeting your needs, STOP. Bring your focus back to the here and now. Then take a step back in your mind and try to figure out where this is coming from. Why am I allowing my thoughts to run wild? Is this what I want to attract into my life? Is this the vibration I want to hold myself to?

Sometimes you will be able to very quickly gain control and move on with your day, and other times you will find it incredibly difficult to shift your mind off whatever is causing you to spin out of control.

In these moments, if you keep doing whatever it is you are doing, your mind will spin out of control and you will find yourself going on a familiar, painful ride. If you completely change everything you are doing -- both physically and mentally – your mind will be forced to refocus on a new activity and stop paying attention to the negative thoughts. Your mind cannot do something different and something the same at the same time. Drop what you are doing and go for a walk. Crank up some good tunes. Get in the car and grab a cup of coffee. Pick up the phone and call a good friend who will hold you to the highest standard you have of yourself. Go window shopping at the mall. Play with the kids at the park. Do anything that will force you to shift your mind.

Once you have regained control, go back and reflect on what just happened. What was the trigger point for that spiral? Once you figure out what the trigger thought was – he was late, she yelled at me -- you can say, 'Okay, if I know I don't like this and if I know that I don't want to react this way or behave in this manner, then what do I want? How do I want to be? How do I want to behave? What do I want the end result to be?' Asking yourself these questions forces the brain to move in a different direction. Every time you force the brain to consider new information, you create a new path for your thoughts to go. Then the next time a habitual, negative thought comes up, you already know where you want your mind to go. You have created a new mind map while at the same time bringing yourself back into harmony with the greater part of you, and that feels good.

No matter what kind of experience or relationship you are in, well-meaning friends, lovers, neighbors, and co-workers are always eager for you to share their pain. People whose thoughts spin out of control need to validate the way they feel. How many times has a friend shared a long, painful conversation with you and when it is over, the friend walks away feeling much better but you feel like you have vomit on you? It is up to you to be clear about where you are and how you want to feel. If you are not clear about how you feel, you will absolutely find yourself taking a ride with them, and it will not feel good. It is up to you to hold your vibration and allow them to catch up with YOU. Negative thoughts, negative ideas, and negative assumptions of others are never your deal unless you make it so.

A friend was weepy and sad at work one day and Lani asked her why. 'I'm turning forty next week,' she said, 'I feel like I haven't done the things I am supposed to do.' Judging, beating herself up, fear ... wow, what a ride she's about to go on. One I am sure she would have been on all week if I hadn't asked her one question: 'What is different about today than yesterday?' She didn't know. 'One thought,' I said, 'and one that doesn't feel good.'

Connecting the dots between thoughts and feelings is a mystery until you know a little bit more about the connection between your brain and your body. Again, Joe Dispenza definitively puts this mystery to rest. Did you know that every time you have a thought, you produce a chemical? And that every chemical your thoughts produce rushes through the bloodstream and into your cells, imme-diately producing a very distinct feeling? Our bodies are like giant pharmaceutical factories that turn on every time we have a thought. Mind-body connection is real.

So every time you have inspired thoughts or happy thoughts, within a matter of seconds you make chemicals that make you feel in-spired or happy. Every time you have negative thoughts or degrading thoughts, within a matter of seconds you begin to feel negative and unhappy. Here's what happens -- every time an unformed thought materializes inside the brain, circuits fire and produce its chemical bio-equivalent, called a neuropeptide. Every thought we have mani-fests into the physical world as a chemical molecule that produces a distinct feeling. You can *feel* your thoughts.

Notice the next time you have a conversation with yourself about you or your life. It either feels good or it feels bad. It either builds you up or tears you down. Not only does every thought feel a certain way, every belief (which is nothing more than a thought you think over and over again) feels a certain way.

> To live the life of your dreams, you must change your conversation to match the vibration you want to hold. Not just the conversations that you know others are listening in on ... ALL of them. Every conversation, every word, every intent must be in harmony with that which you say you want. The moment they are, you will see that which you are wanting to see.
>
> ∽∂∾

So let's say you are driving your car. You begin telling a story to your-self about your mother-in-law, your kids, or the neighbor down the street. As soon as the chemical equivalents of your thoughts hit your bloodstream and find their way into your cells, your brain begins to no-tice that you feel a certain way, and it begins to think the way you feel, which then causes it to release more chemicals for you to feel the way you think, and think the way you feel and feel the way you think until you create a 'state of being' by virtue of the thoughts you are consciously or unconsciously dwelling on.

We do it all the time. We slip in and out of these states of being unknowingly -- and for some, uncontrollably -- every single day.

So let's say, as an example, that over the last six months you have been feeling increasingly productive. You were selected to be part of a decision-making team heading up an important project, and every day for six months you internally measured your productivity against the needs of the project and found ample reason to interpret your actions as productive. So every time you had the notion, 'I was productive today,' you felt a certain way -- let's say, "proud." Would you say that you were creating a state of being by virtue of your thoughts, and those thoughts felt good? Yes. It's simple to understand, when our state of being feels good.

Now let's say six months later you are back in a cramped cubicle crunching numbers. After only a day or two, your internal chatter begins to feel something like this, 'Why wasn't I selected for the next project? I am not appreciated. I hate this. This isn't fun.' By the end of six months sitting at a desk, thinking these thoughts, would you say that you are also unknowingly -- maybe even uncontrollably -- creating a new state of being by virtue of your thoughts? The only difference is that this one does not feel good.

But here is the thing: because neurons that fire together, wire together, the brain doesn't care whether you are thinking good-feeling thoughts or bad-feeling thoughts. Every sub-vocalization that you turn your attention to churns out a chemical bath that creates a feeling that creates a cycle of 'feeling and thinking' and 'thinking and feeling,' and these patterns become automatic sub-programs of thinking that we accept and engage in because we think they are real.

Now let's say you are through with suffering. You get up in the morning and announce, 'Today is the day. Today I am going to stop. Today I am going to be happy. This is my choice. I am going to do all the things that serve me and my personal growth,' and after an hour or so you are right back where you started, wallowing in internal chatter that tears you down. How can this be?

Neurophysiology tells us that every cell in the human body below the brain is a thinking cell. There is no difference between a brain cell and a receptor cell's ability to produce the chemical equivalent of a thought.

This tells us that after years of thinking depressed thoughts or lonely thoughts or unworthy thoughts, the cells of the body have the ability to override our best intentions and send their own message up the spinal column to the brain. And we know this because after only a few hours of declaring, 'I will no longer overeat,' 'I will no longer yell,' and 'I will no longer feel guilty,' we begin to hear sub-vocalizations and internal chatter along the lines of, 'You can start tomorrow,' 'Today is not a good day,' or 'Who do you think you are kidding?'

This is why New Year's resolutions rarely work. Our physical bodies crave 'what is.' Our biology craves the familiar, to the point that the brain is *always* filling in what you see with what it knows, not what we want. Your body, which you have conditioned with chemical baths of your choosing over the years, can and will decide for itself what state of being it prefers. I am overweight. I am unhappy. I am ugly. I am depressed.

We talk ourselves out of greatness because we believe this internal chatter is real. When we tune in to this internal chatter and engage, we really make it real. To truly change means we must think greater than our environment. To truly change takes an act of will.

So how do you pull the mind out of the body and put it back in the brain? By practicing thinking and acting greater than how we feel. We must first decide how we want to feel, and then re-train the mind to find the thought that feels the way we want to feel. This is how you cause the mind and the body to work together to *experience* the change you wish to see. When you get to the point where you choose thoughts based on feeling and not the other way around (suppressing your feelings by your thoughts), you are consciously creating your life, because you are ALWAYS going to pick what feels good.

Repeating an action over and over again teaches the body to think like the brain. Harping on a negative story -- I've had a less than perfect childhood, I don't make enough money, I'm in a horrible re-lationship, the economy is collapsing – teaches the body to feel bad. When thoughts and stories we tell tear us down, they feel like depres-sion, anxiety, anger, confusion, and stress. We are out of alignment with the state of joy and abundance that can be ours for the asking. We are out of alignment with our inner self.

On the other hand, when we choose to focus on a positive story -- I love my life, I am grateful for my job, my parents did the best they could do, I love listening to my children laugh, I see myself in a healthy relationship, I love ME and all that life has caused me to be -- we feel good. These thoughts and stories build us up. They feel like love, hope, joy, passion, enthusiasm, expansiveness, and relief. They make us feel good. We are in alignment with our inner self.

Your inner self is always talking to you in the only language it knows: *feeling*. Let your feelings be your guide.

Every time you feel bad, do not try to think your way out of it. This is you telling you that you are not in alignment with YOU. Every negative thought that you allow yourself to dwell upon keeps you away from what you truly desire to become. Every negative thought holds you in discord from your true self. And if like attracts like, and this is the vibration that you are offering, then this is what you are getting back.

When you feel good, this is the non-physical you telling the physical you that you are in alignment with the greater part of you. You are allowing your thoughts to keep up with what life has caused you to become. You are seeing that which you are giving your attention to through the eyes of the greater part of you. And if like attracts like, this is the vibration that you are offering and this is what you are getting back.

You must be in alignment with the greater part of you to experience the joy and inner peace you seek.

Begin to look for ways to tell a new story about who you are becoming and what is on its way. Change your conversation as you look for ways to feel good. Every chance you get tell stories that are a little more hopeful, a little more possible, a little more of what you are creating. Talk about how wonderful your children are and how you love to see them laugh and play and grow into beautiful beings. Talk about how it will feel to have the things that you are wanting. Pick up on the sense of relief that comes over you every time you talk about the things that you are wanting, things that bring you joy.

Allow yourself to feel your life. How does this relationship feel? How does this person feel? How does this experience feel? You must begin to find new ways to feel differently. Feel your thoughts and let them guide you. Match the words you use and actions you take to the thoughts that feel good or feel better. PRACTICE something different every day -- practice feeling good.

It is good to feel good. It is natural for you to love yourself and your life. It is natural for you to be joyful. It is natural for you to know well-being. It is natural for you to expand. It is natural for you to question and re-choose. It is natural for you to want more.

This is the most authentic communication of all…your feelings!

CHAPTER THREE

LISTEN TO YOUR INNER GUIDANCE

How do you know who you are? How do you connect with YOU? Get quiet and turn off all the chatter going on in your mind. How can you hear yourself if you have conversations of he said, she said, wow that makes me angry, or worries of problems flying around in your head? Take control of your thoughts and what you allow yourself to ponder on. Get to know your Self, love your Self, free you Self!

WHAT IS YOUR INNER GUIDANCE? It is the part of you that never changes, the part of you that has always felt the same – when you were six, when you were eighteen, when you were twenty-nine, and right now. Certainly you have noticed that even as your physical body has grown and matured, there is a part of you that has always felt consistently familiar, a part that has always felt like YOU. That feeling of you, the silent observer, is the non-physical you, the real you, the part of you that talks to you in the only language it knows -- through *feeling.*

Our feelings are a natural part of us. As children we are taught that we have no control over how we feel. Today we know that just the opposite is true. Tuning into how you feel is tuning into YOU, tuning into the greater part of you, communing with the greater part of you. Your job is to listen -- intently listen -- to how you FEEL.

The key to happiness is not things; to be truly happy is to be totally in tune with you -- who you are, what you want, and where you want to be in this lifetime. Giving up or surrendering for something less does not make you happy. It makes you feel empty inside. Giving away bits and pieces of yourself because you feel you must co-create an experience with a difficult person does not make you happy; it doesn't even make the difficult person happy. You can never shovel enough love into a difficult person's heart to fill the hole that exists there. Only that person knows what caused the hole to be there in the first place. Stop trying to fix what you cannot fix, and turn around. Your job is to find what resonates and feels like joy within YOU. It is not your role to make others happy. It is your job to discover and nurture a healthy relationship between you and your inner guide.

Our inner guide is talking to us all the time. One day last summer, Lani was walking into church with a friend. As she held the door open, her friend reached into her purse and pulled out her phone. "Put that thing away," Lani said. "I know, I'm bad," her friend said with a sheepish smile as she walked in.

You know who that was? That was her inner guide, talking quietly.

We all do it. We listen or we don't listen, on all levels of our life. *Change Your Conversation* is about listening to those whispers all the time. It is about paying attention to your inner voice, because that is your inner guide talking to you. It is about practicing self-empowering thoughts that are meaningful to you, because repetition is what the brain needs to keep up with you.

Richness and wealth accompany every emotion. Our emotions are what make us feel alive. And yet, we have been steered away from exploring emotion even though through emotion, we can figure life out. Feelings, impulses, and imagination are all gifts. They are all part of a built-in guidance system that is part of being human. Learn to develop belief systems in accordance with your fundamental nature, and they will steer you in the direction of your greatest growth. We are glorious, joyful beings. Love this body you are in and the way it speaks to you. Trust your feelings and develop your intuition so you completely, and lovingly, create your life.

When you are aligned with your inner self, you cannot help but uplift and inspire those around you. Your value to them is absolutely the amount of joy you radiate and cause others to feel. But the only thing you can give them is your example. It is up to them to observe, then long for, then work out to achieve, what they see in you. Everybody is responsible for the direction of their thoughts and objects of their desire. Everyone is responsible for their greatest growth.

> It's amazing how everything begins to fall right into place when we allow ourselves to become incredibly clear about what we want on every level of lives without allowing the input or expectations of others to get in the way. If we simply tune in, relax, create, and then sit back and allow ourselves to receive, life becomes magical, expansive, and exciting!
>
> ⌒∞⌒

It takes courage to look inside and listen to our own Inner Guidance. Do we dare to be ourselves? That is the question. For some, maybe not in this lifetime. You get to control the way you feel, because you get to choose which thoughts you dwell upon and which to let go. As Abraham says, so many people think their only option is to engage in all the circumstances that surround them. And that is when they attempt the impossible -- which is to control the circumstances around them, which only makes them feel frustrated and vulnerable, because it doesn't take very much life experience to discover that you can't control all of those circumstances. But you can control your vibration.

And when you control your vibration, you control everything that has anything to do with you.

A healthy relationship with your family, your spouse, your children, or friends, begins with you. Allow yourself to have the connection with yourself that you are looking for in others. Love the being that talks to you, respect the being that stares back at you when you look in the mirror, feel the joy radiate from within. When you are one with you, only then can you truly be one with others.

Malinda's Story. "Over the past two weeks my son, who will be three in January, has been a handful, to say the least. No matter what I did, his response to me was to totally fall to pieces. If you have kids, you know what I mean -- I'm talking about the screaming, crying, melting to nothing in the middle of the floor, and I thought I was going to lose my mind. I kept trying different approaches and to no avail, until I decided enough was enough.

"A couple of days prior, I decided it was time to figure out what was really going on with me and my relationship with my son. Understanding that he is only three, I also understand that everything begins and ends with me. It was time to get quiet, take a step back, and take a look at what has really been going on. Very quickly I realized that I had started dreading having time with my son because I didn't want to deal with his tantrums. It was time for me to change my conversation. Once I stepped back and I could see where I had allowed my thoughts to go in a direction that did not feel good to me, I was able to say to myself, 'Now that you know what you don't want, what do you want?' My response was, 'I want a healthy relationship with my son. I want to enjoy my time with him. I want to laugh and play with him.' Suddenly I went from feeling like I was going to lose it at any minute to feeling overjoyed with the love that I feel for my son.

"The next few days were incredibly fun, spending the entire day laughing, playing, building blocks, playing trucks, reading books, Christmas shopping, and watching movies -- without any meltdowns! Once I changed my conversation and let go, a few hours later it hit me that I had not been playing or interacting with my son as much as he might need. I had been so wrapped up in work, Christmas, decorating, and the list goes on, that I wasn't seeing his needs. My outside was reflecting my inside. His behavior was reflecting back to me what I was feeling inside. As soon as I changed my conversation with myself, I connected with me, with my truth, with my real self once again, and I was able to connect with my son again. LIFE IS GOOD!

"The most important relationship of all – your children -- always begins and ends with YOU!

"My life is in constant motion and so are my children. I have come to learn that I have to pay attention to them in the same manner that I pay attention to myself, my work, my house, etc. -- meaning every couple of days I step back and evaluate where they are in relation to where I am. Am I responding to them in a healthy way that feels good to me, or am I just reacting? Are there any new behaviors that need to be addressed and if so, what are the options available to me, and which of those bring me a sense of relief?

"Once I have gotten down to things and have become clear about where I want to move things with my children, the next step is actually putting them into place. This requires me to be totally in the now. This requires me to be totally focused on nothing else but my kids when I am interacting with them. Now that I am aware of behaviors that do not feel good to me, I have to be aware of what triggers those same behaviors so that I can redirect them with love and compassion rather than with anger or disappointment. The key is knowing that it all begins and ends with you.

"If you are reacting out of anger or disappointment, it has absolutely nothing to do with the child, and has everything to do with you. I found when I react out of anger or disappointment it is always because I wasn't totally in the now, because I had a million other things on my plate and expected my child to move at my pace, expected my child to do things the way I wanted them done, expected my child to do what I would have done -- and was not allowing myself to see my child through source's eyes. I also understand that my children reflect back to me the energy that I give to them, as with everything else in life. Our children are no different."

> When you are aligned with your authentic self, you cannot help but uplift and inspire those around you. Your value to them is absolutely the amount of joy you radiate and cause others to feel. But the only thing you can give them is your example. It is up to them to observe, then long for, then work out to achieve. Everybody is responsible for the direction of their thoughts and objects of their desire.
>
> ‿✑‿

Our challenge in this lifetime is to identify and maintain joy, whatever that means to you. In between your mood swings and the drama that swirls around you, your challenge is to find and vibrate and resonate joy. This is how you find your purpose. It is how you think of yourself. When you can feel your inner guide, when you can feel yourself – whatever that means to you – you have found your purpose, because you are now hearing your inner guide.

Remember that you yourself are the center of your being. You are the only one walking around in your life. You carry your power with you in every experience. Joy is a power that nobody can generate, or make go away, but you.

When you feel unsure of yourself or your decisions, or whether you are on the right path, tune into the conversations going on inside your head. Are you going in circles, driving yourself crazy, questioning everything under the sun, and still no answer? STOP. Turn off the chatter and listen to your gut feeling. What is your first reaction? What brings you a sense of relief? The thought that brings a sense of relief is the one to listen to … this is you.

There are those who find tuning into their feelings quite an adjustment after years of not knowing how. At first it takes some time to recognize that you are feeling bad, that you are beating yourself up with the internal conversations you are having with yourself, and that you habitually ignore how you feel. Once you learn that you can manage your thoughts by paying attention to how they make you feel, you can determine how you want to feel, and begin using your feelings to guide and steer you in the direction you know you want to go. Make how you feel a priority above everything else going on in your life. Choose to feel good.

Be clear about the fundamental nature of life. It is ever-evolving. There is a natural ebb and flow. There will always be contrast. It will never stay the same. There will always be downward spirals to test your connection with you. There will always be opportunity to reflect and evolve your life. Your job is to recognize when you are not in a good feeling place and shift your thoughts to bring yourself back into harmony with you.

Moving your energy from negative to positive is a gradual process. Be a little more hopeful. Talk less about what is going wrong and more about what is going right. Foster the attitude of "I am satisfied with what is" and "I am eager for what is to come."

Listen to your Inner Guidance.

How many times have you become complacent or have started to take for granted all that you have around you? Or you look around and don't like what you see, wanting more and not feeling gratitude for what you already have? All of a sudden life throws you a curve ball that makes you look up, and right in front of your eyes your world has changed. You LOVE what you have and couldn't be more grateful for all that has come your way.

Malinda's Story. "I was on the phone chatting with a lady who called to talk about how rough things are. She couldn't seem to pull herself out of a funk that she had been in for a while. She had gotten to a point where she hated the house she lived in, couldn't wait to be able to afford something bigger, couldn't wait to get rid of all her furniture and buy new stuff. And then out of the blue, she received a phone call from a neighbor. Her house was on FIRE! She flew home as quickly as possible to have the fire chief tell her that if her neighbor had not called when he did her house would have burned to the ground!

"She got very quiet on the phone and said, 'Why is this happening to me?'

"My response was, 'This was for you.'

"What do you mean?" she asked.

"I said, 'Can you imagine losing everything, all of your possessions, all of your pictures of your kids, everything you have worked for your entire life?'

" 'NO,' she said, 'I can't. That would be awful.'

" 'Exactly,' I said. 'All of a sudden things aren't so bad, are they? All of a sudden you LOVE your house and all the love that it is filled with. It's your home.'

" 'Be grateful that someone was around to catch the fire before it got out of hand,' I continued. 'Be grateful for this experience that has shown you that your world is not so bad after all.' "

What you think and feel, and what manifests, is a match every single time. She was so focused on how much she hated her house and all of her belongings and wanted nothing more than to get rid of it all and start over, not understanding that that was exactly what she was creating. That was exactly what she had attracted into her life. Now that she has had this contrast, she has a chance to redefine yet again what it is that she truly wants -- this time around with pure gratitude for all that life has given her! She has an opportunity to change her conversation and begin creating a life she loves and a life that she is grateful for.

Have you ever noticed how many times we allow our thoughts to override how we feel? We justify, blame, point fingers, or become righteously indignant. But let's face it: none of these feels good no matter what the thought, reason, or belief. When you use words like "should've," "could've," and "would've," your internal conversation is not present -- it is somewhere in the past, or projecting into the future. Let go of right and wrong so you can objectively look at an uncomfortable aspect of your life. Find a solution that works better and move on.

To learn from a mistake, be brave enough to turn around and look at the entire process leading up to the mistake, wondering every step of the way, how did that feel? How did that feel? Somewhere along the way, LONG before the mistake was made, something did not feel right. THAT was your Inner Guide guiding. THAT was you not listening. Listen to your feelings. They are YOU guiding YOU.

Purify yourself every night.

So how do we listen to our Inner Guidance when there is so much chatter in our head? There are two times during each and every day when we are most in touch with our inner self. The first is when we are just falling asleep – somewhere in between waking and dream state – and the second is when we are just waking up. During both of these transitional times, we pass our inner self most clearly as we move from one state of consciousness to another. During each of these times, your Inner Guide will most definitively allow you to feel the answer you are looking for. It may take a while to settle down and let go of trying to control what you think the answer should be. But once you let go and let your true feelings float into your awareness, you will always "hear" the answer -- not through words, but through an unmistakable feeling of inspiration or relief: a momentary, fleeting sensation that you immediately know to be true.

Transitioning between waking consciousness and dream state is when you and your Inner Guide glide by each other completely, as one. These are the two most uncluttered parts of our day, when we are most alone with ourselves and can truly touch our non-physical self. It is when our inner wisdom speaks clearly and thoughts do not get in the way.

Inner peace is a quiet process of coming into harmony with you. When you allow yourself to focus on thoughts that are aligned with the very core of you, you will notice that amazing things begin to happen. All of a sudden contrast becomes a friend, not an insurmountable hurdle intentionally blocking our way. There is no feeling of lack, only abundance, because we are in touch with our own power and tapped into our ability to control every experience we allow into our lives. We are at peace with ourselves.

Ask yourself every night, "Am I willing to change?" "Am I willing to trust my instincts, listen to my gut, and love myself more than anything or anyone else?" "Am I curious about my own potential?" "Am I willing to explore me?" It has been said that if you always do what you have always done, you'll always get more of what you have always gotten. So today is the day to try something new. Move beyond physical thought and the past, and listen to the part of you that has always been with you and is eagerly waiting to serve.

Find a way to see things in a different light. Make it a point every night before you go to bed to review your day. When you fall asleep at night, do so mindfully. Embrace the stillness as you transition and gently, non-judgmentally, go over your day. Purify it. What thoughts and actions felt good? Which did not feel so good? In order to purify and let things go, you have to get to a place of gratitude. Find a way to look for the lessons throughout the day that made you grow. Look deeply for a sense of relief. Then turn your focus on what you want tomorrow to bring. From there, don't worry about how things are going to get done. Just stay focused on what you want, and know it will happen. Set your intention as you drift off, so when you awaken you have already consciously created your day – exactly as you dream it to be.

CHAPTER FOUR
CHOICE

Gandhi's wife was once asked how he got so much done.
"Because he is congruent in his thoughts, words and actions," she
said. "They are perfectly aligned."

EVERYTHING BEGINS WITH A THOUGHT, every thought has a distinct feeling, and every feeling is YOU talking to you. As you begin to turn your focus more toward what you want, you begin to exercise choice. You begin to choose how you want to feel. In every experience, moment, or conversation there are choices to be made. As you become clear about what you want, who you want to be, and where you want to go, it is easy to allow your inner voice to guide you, because you already know how you want to feel. Yet, we are also choosing even when we allow others to determine how we feel. The key is to choose to feel good about you, which will always resonate as positive emotion, whether you call it joy, inspiration, enthusiasm, love, balance, or peace. When you hold this higher vibration in the conversations you have with yourself and others, this will be the exact feeling you attract into your life.

You are in total control.

You have to choose to feel good, in order to feel good. Whatever that means to you, however that feels to you, you are the only one who can decide how you want to feel. Once you decide, you have to keep deciding to feel good about the events, circumstances, and people that will constantly move in and out of your life. You have to hold the vibration that feels good to you, even though life changes around you.

You are the only one who knows what is right for you. You are the only one who can choose what best serves you. You are the only one who will live your life. In your day-to-day routine, don't forget that YOU are the only one in control. Others may pretend they are in control. Others may entice you to give up control because if they can control the way you feel, they will feel better about themselves. Learn to consult with the greater part of you. Listen to how you feel, and make choices based on how you want to feel. Choose.

Every time you feel challenged, you are being asked to grow just a little bit more. Every time you feel like you are in a bit of a pinch, you are being asked to reach just a little bit more – by the rude driver behind you, by the difficult child on your block, by the co-worker who yells at you, and by the memories that haunt you. There is no one who can tell you what to do. You are the only one who knows what the opposite of these things are that will bring you joy. Demonstrate to yourself that you have the ability to create a life that feels good. Look around at all the things you enjoy. Did you not do these things? Now understand that you can create all of your life to feel the same way. Why would you settle for anything less?

Everything happens just as it should: there is no good or bad, there is only well-being. The bumps in the road and troubling situations we all experience are contrast – simple reminders -- given for you to once again even more clearly define who you are, what your core beliefs are, and where you want to go from here.

Put thought aside. Your choice in every moment of every day is to feel worse or to feel better, to evolve or regress. You always get to choose, and the only way to choose authentically is to relax. Relax and listen to yourself. Stop pushing. Love what you have created thus far, because at some point, it served you. Now choose, and choose again. Choose a higher expression and grander version of what you have already created, because it is what you are always going to do. Do it now, or do it later -- at some point you will move on.

No matter where you find yourself today, every decision you have made along the way, you thought was the right one. People never do things because they think they are wrong. We always do things because we think we are right. Nobody ever wakes up in the morning and thinks to themselves as they brush their teeth, "I wonder how badly I can screw up my day today?"

Instead of judging yourself and beating yourself up, look at the choices you have made in your life and call them your preference at the time. I preferred living with somebody who said they wanted to take care of me. I preferred telling everybody how stupid they are. I preferred dropping out of school. These were preferences at the time, but they do not have to be your preferences now. If you want something different, prefer something different. This is how you choose.

Some of us have allowed others to choose for us for so long that we don't even know how to choose anymore. Do you feel you have a choice? In everything or just some things? Here's the thing -- if you feel you have a choice in ONE thing, it follows that you have a choice with everything. No exceptions. You just have to accept the fact that giving away your ability to choose is a choice, and unfortunately one that usually does not feel good.

Choosing what you think, feel, and speak requires courage -- courage to look over your life (without judgment) and decide what works, what used to work, and what doesn't work anymore. We are taught by the media and "those in power" that we are incapable of deciding what is right for us. We tell you from our vantage point that nobody knows better than you what is right for you. You must rise to a new level of responsibility and honesty in your relationship with yourself.

There are an unlimited number of ways to choose. Your ability to imagine ways for your life to change is a new mind map in the making. The secret is to think less and feel more. If you can feel your choices, you are really looking at them. If you can't feel your choices, you are thinking your life, and all of us know that just because you have a thought doesn't mean it's true. Never unknowingly set yourself up for powerlessness and victimization because you are not clear about how every choice will feel once it is integrated into your life.

What about my family and friends? What if they don't agree with what I want for myself? You have no control over others, any more than they have control over you. Their deal is not your deal, just as your deal is not their deal. Your preferences belong to you. The only person walking around in your life is YOU. You are the only one who can choose what is best for you. Choose what is right for you. Choose what feels good for you. Trust your choices, because you can't help but move toward joy. Some people don't want joy, and some people don't want you to have joy, because it makes them think of the joy they do not have.

If choices of the past caused you not to want to love yourself, you will have a very difficult time loving another, since you'll resent the time and energy you give another person that you aren't giving to yourself. If you choose another's happiness above your own, you will resent what you give away, because it rightfully belongs to you. Every time we pinch ourselves off from our true selves and make choices to try to change others around us, we lose ourselves and are still not happy. Out of all the possibilities that you see, always choose what feels good to YOU. Always choose to be happy!

Life demands our attention, so when there are matters at hand that need to be addressed, take the time to step back, clear your mind of all the chatter concerning the issue, get quiet, and feel your way through to a sense of relief instead of allowing yourself to spin. Tune out all the voices of friends and family, and listen to YOU. This is where you get to choose to harness your power or give it away. Make every decision from the core of your being, YOU.

When we say, "do not give away your power" or "practice self-empowerment," we are talking about maximizing your ability to make choices that best serve you. This is not magic. This means you must pay attention to your life. You must pay attention to you, because if you don't observe the variety around you and the possibilities that surround the variety, who will?

Do not buy into the myth that there is only one way. Do not allow yourself to become rigid and

> The connection between small ideas and big ideas is very important. Every big idea -- whether it be a undesirable drama or an amazing creation -- starts with a single, small thought, and this is important, because at that moment you always have the ability to continue, to re-direct -- or avoid altogether -- its expansion.
>
> ↝∾

unyielding in your thinking. This is a common affliction that causes many to shut down and settle within the confines of a singular belief system, typically somebody else's belief system. The universe is expansive, vast, and never-ending. Anything is possible; all things are possible, if you can imagine it, you can have it. You are part of an expansive, vast, and never-ending universe. The possibilities are endless, if you believe there has to be a better way.

Whether you are in a relationship or not, whether you have a family or not, you are on this journey alone. So many times we put ourselves in bad relationships or make not-so-great choices because we are afraid of being alone. You are alone. You are the only one walking your path. You are the only one who can make the choices that lie before you. You are the only one who knows what is best for you. Harness your power rather than push it away! And when you choose, choose because you want to. Choose it all.

Let's put this into real terms. Let's say, for instance, that you are at work. A huge hurdle shows itself and you have to come up with a solution … and quickly. Immediately you begin brainstorming, and several options come to mind. You begin to work through the first one. Nope, that won't work. Quickly you move on to the second one. Not that one either. You work through the third one and the fourth one and continue working different scenarios in your mind, all the while staying focused on the end result – what you want. You may call upon co-workers to contribute different opinions for the same solution. All of this is called data collection – moving through endless possibilities before landing on the one that FEELS good, the one that brings a sense of relief.

Learning to work through different scenarios for yourself, your life, your relationships, and your money always means the same thing – thoughtful consideration of all possibilities with the intent of landing on the one that brings a sense of relief. You are always looking for a feeling, never a thought. Feeling comes first, thought comes second. It is your job to identify the thought or scenario that brings a sense of relief and a radiant and expansive burning in your core. This is how you choose the path that serves you best.

Sometimes finding a sense of relief when you are in the middle of a difficult situation is not easy. This is when you intentionally practice being patient, when you give up linear time, when you relax, get quiet, turn off all of the internal chatter, and trust that when the solution comes to you, you will recognize it and move on.

Pausing, relaxing, not judging yourself, and allowing an answer to come is intentionally wanting to see things the way your inner guidance sees it too. You are pausing and waiting for the undeniable sense of relief that means YOU are connected with the greater part of YOU. Sometimes this feels like a burning within the core of your being. Sometimes, it is a sensation like your heart is about to pop out of your chest. Every time, however, you have a sense of knowing. Slow down and turn your attention to it. This is the feeling you are looking for: a strangely familiar, connected feeling within the very core of your being that you know is there. When you feel it, stop. Look at it. This is YOU creating. This is YOU connecting. This is you moving your life in a direction that you really want to go.

You are always going to be the only one who knows what is right for you. You are the only one who can choose what best serves you. You are the only one who will ever live your life. Make a commitment to yourself to unfold every opportunity, to look be-

hind every closed door, to turn over every stone along the way. Look for opportunities to move you closer to where you want to be.

Make a commitment to yourself.

Your brain is your best friend, after you choose because the brain does not know the difference between practicing and doing. This is why thinking about what you want, visualizing what you want, daydreaming and imagining what you want, works. Too many experiments prove it.

In *Evolve Your Brain*, Dispenza tells of an interesting experiment with four groups of people and a piano. Functional brain scans were performed on each person participating in the experiment before it took place. Shortly afterward, each person was asked to do a couple things with a piano; then another functional brain scan was done to see if any measurable differences had taken place.

The first group was told, we are going to show you a number of scales and chords. Pay attention and practice on the piano – physical- ly rehearse – for two hours a day for five days. As you would expect, at the end of five days, they re-scanned their brains and saw a whole new set of circuits on one side of the brain.

The second group was told, come and play whatever you want for two hours a day for five days. They rescanned their brains and there was hardly any change. Why? With no new information, they couldn't repeat what they did the day before because they couldn't remember what they did and they weren't paying attention because there were no instructions, so they couldn't repeat any new thought over and over. Their brains grew only slightly.

The third group was told, don't even show up. What do you think happened? Nothing happened, which means if you don't have new experiences, you don't learn anything new, your brain doesn't change.

The last group was told, instead of physically playing scales and chords, memorize the scales and chords, mentally rehearse in your mind playing the scales and chords. Don't even show up. At the end of five days, the fourth group grew the same amount of circuits as the people who physically demonstrated the scales and chords. These people changed their bran just by thinking in new ways. When the brain is truly focused and paying attention, it does not know the difference between what is happening out there and what is happening in here.

You don't need a piano to visualize a new way of thinking, new ideas, new goals, or a new life. Visualization can take place in your car, at home, at work, even during REM and non-REM sleep. Recent studies on dreaming and sleep-state consciousness demonstrate that REM sleep is an internal mirror of the real world. In non-REM sleep, the brain takes the past and tries to figure out how that might relate to the future. In REM sleep, the brain actually tries to experience the future by moving into the future. REM-state dreams are simulations to test possibilities. Pay attention to your dreams. They are a reflection of your waking-consciousness state.

The beauty of REM sleep is that, as humans, we can step into the future with no risk in this physical world and open ourselves to the possibilities of reaching our potential, whatever that may be. REM sleep allows us to think outside the box. In 1844, for instance, Elias

> Do you wonder if you are on the right path? Every individual is on their own path, and every path can be made into the right path as you incrementally, and constantly, cause it to reflect whatever truth you say your purpose is founded on.
>
> ◡◠◡

Howe had a vision of the first sewing machine – specifically, how to hold the thread in the needle -- during a dream state. The last thing he remembered upon waking was dreaming of cannibals and their spears, which had a hole in them.

The Periodic Table was realized by Dimitri Mendelev during a dream. Two Nobel Prizes were the results of REM sleep. Innumerable novels, films, and works of visual art have been the result of REM sleep. Medical breakthroughs have been inspired during REM sleep. The key is to control your awareness of your dreams immediately upon waking.

Choice has a lot to do with what you believe. Because the brain is programmed to reinforce only what it already knows, it cannot "see" new opportunities unless you believe they are there. As Wayne Dyer says, "You will see it when you believe it."

To illustrate this point, when Christopher Columbus and his three ships -- the Niña, the Pinta, and the Santa Maria -- pulled into the bay of the Americas, the indigenous people could not see the ships from the shore. They had never seen a white man's ship before, and the image did not register in their minds. But the shaman, noticing ripples in the water, stood on the shore for days, curious as to what was causing this strange activity. Suddenly, the ships materialized. As soon as the shaman saw the ships, everyone else could too.

Who you are is made up of the reality you are currently in. People, places, events, and things that constitute your life are your reality. To change is to change one of those things that constitute your current reality -- a person, place, event or thing -- something most people find hard to do. You are the reality you are creating, because reality is created in the mind.

ᴖᴖᴖ

So what does being happy mean to you? What does feeling good mean to you? Being curious about the possibilities for your life causes the brain to work in new ways. What would it feel like to be happy? What would it feel like to be a happy person? Self-examination is mind in action. Mind in action causes the brain to work.

Without new knowledge, without curiosity, without possibilities, your brain will continue to use only 10% of its power. Your brain will just keep churning out the minute slice of life it already knows. Learn new information. From this new information, see new possibilities. The minute you can physically demonstrate new information in your life, you make it real. Do these things, and you grow new brain circuits. Do these things, and you change your life.

The real question you need to ask yourself every day is: what do you mentally rehearse all day long? What do you physically demonstrate? Because how you act – and how you think -- is who you are, on a neurological level.

If you keep rehearsing the same old conversations, actions, and thoughts in your mind, then you end up with the same old results over and over again, just with different faces, places, and circumstances and the same lessons that you choose not to learn. Once you learn to step back, look for the lessons and start to learn how to make wiser choices based on how you feel, you take mind one step further. You now have the opportunity to use every circumstance in your life to learn how to create a new mind map, a better feeling mind map. You now have good information to think differently and act differently before a difficult event appears again.

Your brain always picks up where it left off. So does everyone else's. In other words, if you left the office yesterday feeling out of sorts with a co-worker, when you arrive today those feelings will dominate your vibration UNLESS you choose a new mind map before you get there. When you choose to shift -- when you choose to identify and hold a better-feeling thought -- everyone and everything shifts with you. Like magic.

One of the biggest battles we as humans seem to face is the one of allowing ourselves to put ourselves first, before anything and everything. When we don't put ourselves first we feel lost, confused, guilty, tired, and resentful. This is because you are making your choices for someone or something rather than for your SELF. Begin making choices for YOU and feel love, passion, expansion, growth, fulfillment, satisfaction, and peace.

This seems so hard because it goes against everything we have been taught from childhood on up through our adult years. Just think of it this way, if you have been taught to think and act the way that you do, then you have the power to teach yourself a new way to think and act. The fun part is that you get to choose, and when you do you will shift, and others around you will shift right along with you.

The moment you decide to let go of everyone's expectations, stop worrying about how someone else will be affected, stop worrying about how things will work out, and start focusing on what would be the desirable outcome for you on all levels, you put the law of attraction to work for you.

So if you know that your boss has a way of tweaking you, upsetting you, and as an end result you end up incredibly angry, use this memory to create a new mind map. When you are ready, go back and look at all of the experiences you have had with your boss with fresh eyes. Look at them with no judgment, no blame, no righteousness, no justification or pointing of fingers. What do you see? Is there a better way to handle the situation? Is there a solution that FEELS better to you? When you start asking these questions, you allow space for other possibilities to come to mind. Work your way through each and every one of them until you have found one that brings with it a sense of relief. Now when you go back to work and interact with your boss, one of you has changed. You have a new thought – or mind map – in place. He will continue to recreate the same event again. This time, however, YOU will respond differently. You have empowered your-self with new knowledge to change the past before it re-creates itself again. That's power.

Changing the way you perceive the events and circumstances of your life is how to replace old habitual thought that no longer serve you with new thoughts that do. You can do this all the time. Begin to move through each day intentionally looking for habits or reactions that no longer serve the new you. Make time in the evening to go back and build a new "mind map" for something better. Visualization works.

A study was done with two groups of people on the effects of vi-sualization. One group was asked to pull a weighted spring for thirty minutes a day. Over time, muscle strength increased 30% over a set period of time. The second group was asked to mentally rehearse pulling the same weighted spring for thirty minutes a day over the same period of time. Muscle strength increased an amazing 22%.

You are what you mentally rehearse every single day – from deal-ing with your kids, to what you put in your mouth, to how you spend your money. When you develop the ability to consciously choose how you want to feel from the moment you wake in the morning, you give yourself permission to create a new day. You have the ability and the opportunity and new knowledge to set the tone for every bit of your day.

Your world is in your words. Look around you right now. What words would you use to describe your life? What words would you use to describe YOU? Do you like the words that come to mind? If not, with great determination, choose better-feeling words. This is the power of conversation.

CHAPTER FIVE
BUILDING A NEW MIND MAP

Relax. Allow yourselves to be. Do not continually project yourself in anticipation of what lies ahead. We call that worry. Be present in every experience. You do your greatest work with yourself because you are your primary tool, and your work is through your thoughts and your understanding of these thoughts. A life well-lived is all about coming to the core of your own ideas about yourself.

> "When we buy into disapproval, we are practicing disapproval. When we buy into harshness, we are practicing harshness. How sad it is that we become so expert at causing such unnecessary harm to ourselves and others. The key is to practice gentleness and letting go."
> ~ Pema Chondron

SO HOW DO YOU GET there? How do you start looking at your thoughts, feeling your feelings, listening to your Inner Guide, and making better choices in everyday life? How do you create a state of being that serves you, complements you, and expresses your core beliefs?

From experience, we will tell you that you can't tackle it all at one time. It has taken time for you to develop the patterns of thinking that you now want to change. It has taken time to manifest the life that currently surrounds you. It will take time to let go of old, familiar thoughts and develop new ways of looking at your life. Do not be discouraged. Be present in every moment. Life is a process, not an event. Be patient, compassionate, and understanding with yourself.

So many times we are understanding, good listeners, compassionate, and patient with everyone else -- including complete strangers -- and yet we don't practice these same feelings toward ourselves. Make a commitment to yourself that you WANT to feel good, that you WANT to experience the powerful, creative ability of your mind. Do it for YOU!

With that said, self-forgiveness is difficult. We are so hard on ourselves -- our parents were hard on us, our teachers were hard on us, the media is hard on us. Look around, everywhere you turn we are told imperfection is unforgivable, that wherever we are isn't good enough. We should do better! No wonder we find it difficult to be kind to ourselves, to forgive ourselves when we did not know better. We need our own kindness. We need to see ourselves for who we are -- we ARE imperfect, and yet we are always willing to learn. Life is full of mistakes because they cause the unfolding of our own self-discovery. Mistakes, or contrast, are how we learn.

So where do you begin? How do you learn to use contrast as a guide, instead of an enemy?

Start at the top. Look at the big, big things around you one by one as you work your way down to the foundation, the very core of your being. Begin with your house and home, your bank account and job, your spouse, your children, co-workers, family, and friends. Ask yourself, how do these feel? How do these feel? As you massage each one into the feeling-place you prefer, space will open up in your mind to begin looking at more and more subtle aspects of your life.

It is difficult to hear your inner voice when you are distracted by a lousy job, a broken-down car, a mortgage you can't afford, or a failing marriage. And don't kid yourself: TV, cell phones, computers, shopping, and drinking are all distractions to avoid being alone. This noise keeps you from knowing YOU. So take care of the loudest noises first. Then relax and settle in. Your life is a *process*. Every new thought you choose to allow into your awareness is YOU building a new mind map for you along the way.

The more that you find resolution with, and let go of, loud, noisy distractions in your life, the more your mind will settle into what is going on right here, right now. When your mind is present – and not jumping backwards or forwards in time -- the more room you *consciously* have to integrate new thought, new growth, new experience, new ideas, new beginnings, new desires, and new inspirations. Start looking at every area of your life. Is this where you want to be? No? Then where do you want to be? What do you really want? Most of us can't answer these questions because we've never asked them *of ourselves* before. We have gotten really good at telling the stories of what we don't want. Turn around and ask, What do I want to become?

When you realize that something in your life is not as you wish it to be, this is an important first step. But it is the next step that means more: identifying what you want to replace the not-so-good-feeling event, person, or circumstance with. You cannot change your life if you don't know what you are changing it to. You have to have a better feeling thought to replace the one you let go. It is that simple.

So when you find yourself angry, upset, confused, hurt, or disappointed with someone or something, ask yourself why? Why am I upset? Why am I disappointed? Asking why breaks down an idea or expectation that we have placed on someone or some-

thing else. In most cases, these are misplaced expectations and we suffer because we are holding onto an unrealistic idea rather than letting it go and coming face to face with what is going on inside of us. Asking "why" is about YOU.

Everything in life you have attracted by the decisions and choices you have made in the past. Everything on every level is your creation. Take responsibility, own it, learn from it, and evolve with it. Whatever you spend your time thinking about is quite literally causing a future event. When you are worrying, you are creating. When you are loving, you are creating. When you are appreciating, you are creating. In every moment ask yourself: what am I creating?

Learning how to control your thoughts takes time. Be patient with yourself. Most behaviors are habitual, learned over time, which means that just as you have practiced throughout your life to be, do, and think the way you are, you have the ability to choose to be, do, and think differently. You have the ability to create new habits, new learned behaviors, a new you.

Being true to yourself is easier than you think; many times we think it is far more difficult than it really is. If you continually make choices that go against who you are and what you believe to be true, you create a life of misery, disappointment, anger, depression, guilt, and jealousy around you. How can that be easier than choosing to create a life of gratitude, joy, inspiration, peace, or love?

Creating a new mind map is simply looking for more ways to feel excited again, free again, joyous, expansive, and giving again.

Purify your space, at home, at work, and in your car. Get rid of anything that does not feel good to you. Start putting quotes that resonate with you on every cabinet door in your kitchen or your bathroom mirrors. Surround yourself with books, articles, and uplifting words of empowerment everywhere. Put them in your bedroom, bathroom, and kitchen. Listen to audiobooks or watch DVDs about self-empowerment and personal growth. Expect to see the change that you wish to see.

Let's Begin

OVER THE NEXT FOUR WEEKS, begin exploring your thoughts so you learn how to reconnect with you. Make a commitment to yourself to change your conversation, change your vibration, and change your life. It begins by building a new mind map.

Week 1
Becoming Aware of Your Thoughts.

What do you think about all day?
Do you control the amount of attention you give to a thought?
Do you let your thoughts wander and spiral out of control?

By making thoughts visible, you can reflect upon the tone, the intent, and the energy each thought offers. Whenever we have a thought we have the ability to pause, step back, and choose to pay attention to it or not. When we choose to go with a thought, that thought becomes a string of continuous thoughts that turns into a conversation we have with ourselves. And since EVERY conversation we have with ourselves either builds us up or tears us down, it makes sense that in order to feel good about our lives, we must pay attention to how our conversations feel.

Get to know you.

This week notice how thoughts become things by looking at the words you use and the conversations you have with yourself and others.

Each night before you go to bed, grab a pen and notebook, and with no judgment write down all of the thoughts you can remember spending any time thinking about throughout your day. The purpose of this exercise is to become aware of which thoughts you currently give the majority of your attention to. Be honest. Write it down. Look for patterns of thinking. Look for trigger points for downward spirals. Listen to the conversations you have with yourself and others. Listen to the stories you tell.

Purify your space.

Find quotes or uplifting words of empowerment that resonate with you. Surround yourself with them. Place daily reminders or affirmations all around you. Change your screen saver to a marquee of one of these quotes, tape them to your kitchen cabinets, your bathroom mirror, put them in your office as a daily reminder. Every time you see them, focus on how they make you feel. Make it a point to remind yourself on a daily basis to change your conversation.

Practice changing your conversation.

Start practicing a new way of thinking. Start practicing becoming aware of your thoughts. Listen to your conversations, both inside and out. Listen to the vibration that you are holding yourself to. Start becoming aware of where you allow your thoughts to go. Become more in tune with you. Practice, practice, practice, and practice some more. Practice makes perfect.

Week 2
How Do You Feel?

Want to experience thought through feeling?
This week, instead of asking yourself what you think about all day, take this question one step further.
"How do I feel all day?"

If you experience negative feelings during the day, do a quick check. Are your thoughts wandering in the past or projecting worry into the future? Do your thoughts spiral out of control? If the answer is YES, then begin to differentiate between thoughts that no longer exist, thoughts that may never happen, and thoughts that reflect the reality of your life, right here, right now. In other words, be present.

Tune into your thoughts and recognize how they make you feel.

Continue writing your thoughts down without judgment or censorship. This week, organize your thoughts by feeling. Create two columns in your notebook for thoughts that feel good and thoughts that feel bad. Skip a line between each one. Become increasingly aware of how each thought makes you feel. Become more aware of the amount of attention you are giving to each of these thoughts, and how you feel overall. Turn your attention inward. This is the beginning of quieting your mind. This is the beginning of getting to know yourself and who you really are, independent of the good opinion of others.

Be the powerful creator you are meant to be.

Look at every experience you write about as a lesson waiting to be learned. Find a gift that evolves you. Be grateful, and let it go. Open up space in your mind for new thought by changing your conversation. Continue to tell your story differently. "I am in the process of … " "Things are beginning to … " "I am beginning to feel better about … " Continue listening in on the conversations you have with yourself and others, and become increasingly aware of how every conversation makes you feel.

Purify your space and practice.

Week 3
Focus on What You Want

Tune in.

As you continue to write your thoughts down without judgment or censorship, as you continue to organize your thoughts by feeling, go back to where you have skipped a line between each thought and write a new, better feeling thought to replace the old one with.

If you wrote, "I never get things right," replace it with, "I am becoming proficient at my job," "I am learning a new skill," "I am excited about the opportunities this situation affords me."

If you wrote "I'm broke," replace it with, "I am surrounded by an infinite source of abundance," "I am open to new opportunities for more income," "Money flows generously to me."

Feel how each new thought opens you up. Feel how each new thought changes the way you feel. Hold that vibration by visualizing what that new thought brings to you. Close your eyes and begin to see it, touch it, and feel it. Open up to unseen possibilities. Whether you call it brainstorming, daydreaming, or wishful thinking, you want to replace old thoughts that tear you down with new thoughts that move you closer to where you want to be. You will always know you are on the right path when you feel a sense of relief. When you feel a sense of relief, immediately look for the thought that brought it. Let your feelings guide you. Feel your thoughts, allow your mind to wander, trust your gut, and courageously move forward into new uncharted territory. Be willing to know more.

As you become aware of your thoughts, you may begin to see that you have misplaced expectations all over the place. As each experience surfaces, take the time to re-evaluate and look at it with new eyes. Take that opportunity to once again revisit your core beliefs. Is this what I truly believe? Is this what I see as a healthy relationship? Is this being kind and compassionate? Is this what I want to attract and manifest in my life? If I know I don't want this, then what do I want? Continue to take every opportunity to work on building a new mind map -- one experience and one conversation at a time.

Purify and Practice.

Week 4
Vision Boards

Holding onto a new, better-feeling thought is much easier when you keep all of your goals and dreams in front of you. To keep your new mind map in front of you, use a dry erase board. Write your goals and dreams on it. Read them every day. Read them many times a day. Continually remind the brain where you want it to go. If you give your brain direction, it will obediently follow. If you don't, it will pick up right where it left off and leave you feeling defeated and confused.

The brain is meant to serve you, not master you. This is how you begin training your brain to think only about what you want, and how to stay focused on the end result, what you want, so it will come.

Your first board might look something like this:

WHAT DO I WANT?   HOW DOES THAT FEEL?
Me?
Kids?
Marriage?
House?
Car?
Job?

Begin asking yourself core question: Is this where I want to live? Does this place feel good to me? Do I love my surroundings? Am I financially secure? Are my finances in order? Am I happy with the home that I have provided for my children? Am I living my core beliefs? What are my true core beliefs? Is this what I think a relationship should be? What do I want for me? What would bring me peace? Who am I?

Each day, continually come back to the dry erase board, redefining, writing and becoming a bit more clear. You have to see it, touch it, and feel it as if you are truly living it before you can have it. Allow yourself to dream, then verbalize that dream. What would it feel like to have what you truly want, down to the finest of details? Allow yourself to imagine and explore, then create.

Your next board might look something like this:

I AM	I WANT
Courageous	To find true happiness within myself.
Loving	To love myself and all that I have become.
Giving	To connect with my true authentic self.
Caring	To buy my first house within a year.
Strong	To be promoted at my job.
Independent	To make $100,000.00 this year.

Just as you plan out your entire day at work, times for meetings, what needs to be addressed, problem-solving, finding a solution, and putting it into action, do the same for you, for your life. Plan out exactly what you want by how you want each aspect of your life to feel. Take time to address the issues at hand, observe from an objective view, problem-solve, find a solution, and put it into action. This is how you promote yourself. This is how you stay focused on personal growth.

Vision Statement

Take the time to create a vision statement. This is another way to move your thoughts beyond what is, and help you to become more clear about your direction in life on all levels. Check out Dream Manifesto - awesome and worth watching! http://www.dreammanifesto.com/videoclips-intention This will give you a great start!

CHAPTER SIX
THE POWER OF CONVERSATION

Stop running around looking for a solution. It is much simpler than that. Look around you. Decide what parts you want. Decide what parts you do not want. Then trust yourself to be able to rework what is around you into what you want when the opportunity arises. You just have to keep thinking about what you want so you recognize every opportunity when you see it.

> Being aligned with yourself simply means allowing the environment around you to become background noise because you are always tuned into the environment inside of you that vibrates at a higher frequency.
>
> ༄

EVERY STORY YOU TELL MATTERS. Every story either builds you up or tears you down. Every story either brings you into harmony with the non-physical side of you, or not. Every story either allows, or resists, that which you say you want.

So many times we choose to harp on what we don't want: I don't have enough money, I'm broke, I've had less than a perfect childhood, my dad left, my mom left, I was abused, my kids are out of control, my boss hates me, my husband doesn't help me, my wife gripes all the time, I hate my job, I hate school ... the list goes on and on. If our conversations tell us exactly what vibration we are offering to the universe, and if like attracts like, then every time you talk about what you don't want, you get more of what you don't want. We agree with Abraham when they say every negative conversation is you saying, "Come to me, this thing I do not want."

Once you understand that you are in full control of what you allow yourself to dwell on, you will begin to notice that much of what you do not want is rooted in the past or the future. Do you spend a great deal of time beating yourself up over past experiences? Then it is time to find a new way of looking at the same things. Every experience in this lifetime is for YOU, and you alone. What this means is that every experience helps you discover who you are, examine who you are, redefine who you are, and appreciate who you are. This is how you become strong. This is how you become wise. Every experience offers you contrast to become more clear about how far you want to go, how much you want to do, and who you want to be.

The Asking. "I don't want to do the same thing in relationships that I've always done. My relationship with my dad growing up was nonexistent, and I find myself in relationships that are hurtful, painful, and match my relationship with my dad."

Malinda. "Now you know what you don't want. This is the conversation you keep having with yourself and everyone else around you. And so if our conversations are telling us what vibration we are offering, what vibration are you offering? What you don't want! And if like attracts like, then you are getting exactly what you don't want. You've gotten real good at telling that story, and so now we have to flip that story around. You have to start talking, with yourself and everybody else, about what you DO want. All the time. So when you're sitting down with your girlfriend and you're talking, instead of harping on all that you don't have, all the pain you have experienced, all the hurtful things that have been said, turn the conversation around to sound something like: I really want a great guy. I really want a great relationship. I really want to be happy. I really want … fill in the blanks.

"You have to change your conversation. Without changing your conversation, you are not changing your vibration that you are offering. You can think it all day long, but what you are feeling is I don't want, I don't want, I don't want. And so you continue on the vicious cycle of receiving everything that you don't want and everything that matches your dad.

"You have to find the gift that your dad left you, how he empowered you. How he made you who you are today. Be grateful for that, and let it go! Let it go; it's not here anymore. He is not in your life anymore. That is behind you. Be here, right here, right now. What do you want?"

The Asking. "My father was very abusive to my mother when I was a child, and my mom left him. I didn't see him again until well into my adult life. It's just been one of those nonexistent relationships. I've been trying to work on that a lot. I'm going in a few months to visit him for the first time. It has always been in my head that I want to meet my dad, know my dad, and have a relationship with my dad. Even though when I go I may not receive the relationship that I am looking for … I can't change him."

Malinda. "Stop right there. No, you cannot change him. You can't change anyone any more than they can change you. However, you can change your conversation. Talk only about what you want. What you think, feel, and what manifests is always a match … always! If the possibility isn't there now, it will be, if you do your job and only talk about what you want.

"So start over, you're going to visit your dad in a few months, and what do you want? You want a relationship with him. You want to sit down and talk. You want to enjoy him. You want to have a great time. You want to reconnect. You want to meet family that you've never met before. You want to feel loved. You want to feel accepted. You want to be a part of him.

"How does that feel? It feels REALLY GOOD, and you can feel the shift within yourself. That is what you harp on. That is where you stay focused. It doesn't matter what anybody else says. It doesn't matter what anybody else does. It doesn't even matter what he does. You stay focused on you and what you want. And what you think and feel, and what manifests, will always match ... every single time."

When you change your conversation, you are going to dig deep and find a different meaning in all the experiences that you perceive held you back over the years. For some, there are so many that we don't know where to begin. Begin with the ones that weigh you down. Instead of asking, "Why did this happen to me?" begin answering, "Why did this happen FOR me? What is it that I am supposed to be learning from this? What lessons are being offered to me on a huge golden platter? What gift will cause me to expand into an even greater version of who I think I am?"

Asking a different question allows you to take the life experiences that feel bad and flip them around so they feel good. Look at them from a different perspective – objectively, with no judging, no justifying, no defending, no pointing fingers, no emotion -- so you can find a lesson that builds you up; then you can let it go. Allow yourself to take a step back and observe your life from a higher point of view, like you do for your friends. You know, when you're standing on the sidelines watching a friend go through a tough time and you see exactly what is going on and what needs to be done and yet your friend can't seem to see what you see? You gently offer a different point of view that helps your friend very quickly find the right path of action, something that allows them to move past the contrast and get on with their life. We can do the same thing for ourselves if we allow ourselves to find new meaning. The key is learning how to learn. Learn to look for lessons instead of pain.

In Barbara De Angelis' book, *How Did I Get Here?*, she says, "Truth is patient. It will stand outside your door and knock, knock, knock until you let it in." That truth, your lessons, are in every experience in your life. Have you ever wondered why you keep going through the same things over and over again? It may be in different events, people, or places, but it is still the same old scenario over and over again. It has to do with truth – your truth – waiting to be let in.

There are no mistakes, only lessons. Growth is a process of trial, error, and experimentation. As many of you know, lessons are repeated until they are learned. And when you have learned it, you will go on to the next lesson. It never ends. There is no part of life that will not challenge you to reach for the next lesson, to expand and evolve into more of who you are. You must keep up with yourself! There will always be lessons as long as you are alive.

This is where people begin to pick and choose. This is where they learn lessons that are convenient but run away from those that sting. There is no picking and choosing which experiences apply to you and which don't. EVERY experience in your life teaches you more about YOU. The greater the challenge, the greater the growth. Be open to contrast in your life. It always holds another piece of you.

So many times we want to say, "Magic Genie, eliminate all that limits me. Boom! I am free!" This is a classic example of wanting to bypass our feeling center. To let go of something that does not feel good, you must deal with the emotion that put it there in the first place. You have to feel yourself letting go of an unwanted thing. You have to feel a sense of relief.

That sense of relief is buried in the closet where you have also buried your pain. Look at each experience as it comes up. Look for where you have allowed yourself to be led by misplaced expectations or misguided thinking. You will begin to clearly see where you

> Create new stories.
> When you tell the same story over and over, you miss opportunities to move your life. So when you tell an old story, tell it a little bit differently each time. Use every story you tell to move on.
>
> ⌒∂⌒

have allowed yourself to take on others' junk, where you have allowed yourself to become in-volved with problems that you did not cause and can never cure, and where you have not taken care of yourself. We habitually place responsibility for our happiness on others. What a big burden to place on anyone! How can anyone possibly know what would make YOU happy if YOU don't know what makes you happy? Most of us don't even know who we are without the labels we collect and carry around for ourselves: wife, husband, child, mother, caregiver, homemaker, homeowner, leader, or follower. Find what moves the core of your being and you will connect with your true inner self.

Begin to use the contrast in your life as a guide. Refocus. When you know what you don't want, you ALWAYS know what you do want. Without contrast there would be no growth, no expansion, no new desires, no fresh ideas, no inspiration to do better, to have more, or to be someone else.

It always comes back to you. Everything begins and ends with you. Allow yourself to find the gift of every experience -- the gift of personal growth, the gift of knowing yourself even better than before, the gift of becoming wise. When you embrace how life is able to cause you to grow and become more of who you are, you can be grateful for everything you have learned. You can be grateful for the contrast that caused you to see a new path. You can be grateful for the gentle push that helped you choose, yet again, what you really want out of life. And once you feel such gratitude, you can let the contrast go. There is nothing left to hold on to. You have found your gift. You have found your lesson. You have found peace – and a sense of relief -- from within.

Life is experience. The next time you recognize yourself in an uncomfortable event, attempting to communicate with a difficult person, or engaging in a conversation that clearly does not serve you, ask yourself one simple question, "What is the lesson in this for me?"

Let's face it, if we have to suffer through a bitter co-worker, a nasty commute, or a thoughtless blunder, it might as well be for a reason: a reason that helps us respond better next time, deepens our understanding, or practices compassion for others who unknowingly steer a painful boat. Every experience will serve you if you let it.

Malinda's Story. "There are some people in this world who will never get it, and if given the opportunity they will suck the life out of you if you allow them to. You know what I'm talking about -- the kind of person who will try to manipulate you, back you into a corner with their words and actions, and try to make their twisted world yours. I just had an experience with this today, and I have to tell you that it took a great deal of focus on my part to not allow myself to get caught up in the game that was being played. I had to take a moment, remove myself from the room, pull my thoughts together, and re-align myself before going back to engage.

"To re-align myself, I very quickly ran through the situation in my mind and asked myself, 'Where do I want to steer this boat? What options are available to me? And, what do I want out of this?' Because no matter what the other person is saying or doing, I am still in control. I still get to choose on what level I am going to engage or not. I still get to choose if I even want to participate with this person or not.

"Once I decided what option FELT the best to me, meaning it brought me the sense of relief that I was looking for, I returned. In this particular situation I chose to engage on my level. I chose to keep myself in harmony with what I thought was the best way for me to handle this situation without feeling the need to be angry or upset. I chose to not engage on his level. I chose to totally dismiss any comments that were rude or inappropriate. I chose to move past 'what is.' I had to come to the realization that this person will never change, he has always been the same, and that no matter how much I have tried to help him see a better way, he just doesn't get it and that is NOT my deal. By letting go of the 'idea' of how I think this person should be, I freed myself to see things for exactly what they are and at that point, allowed myself to let go and move past the experience to bring about the end result that is in harmony with me, with what I want.

"By the end of the experience, the person who was trying to manipulate me found himself feeling very uncomfortable with me and left! You see, once I decided what I wanted out of the situation and held myself to that vibration, he quickly realized that he was no longer getting under my skin. He no longer had the upper hand. He simply no longer could play the same game he's been playing for years. He really wasn't sure how to act, so he simply picked up his coat and said, 'I have to leave now.'

"And I got what I wanted. I wanted this person to remove himself from my presence without it being a massive blow-up. I wanted this person to leave peacefully. I wanted to feel good about how I chose to engage with this person. I wanted to hold myself to the highest standard of myself that I knew I wanted to be … and I DID! No matter what ball is being thrown at you, always remember that you choose to catch it or not!"

In Mahayana Buddhism, *lojong* means "mind training." Lojong teaches that we can use our difficulties and problems to awaken our hearts. Rather than seeing unwanted aspects of our life as obstacles, we can train our mind to use these raw materials to awaken genuine compassion for ourselves and others. The first step is a willingness to stand fully in your own shoes. The second is to never give up on yourself.

When does this great understanding happen? When YOU decide you don't want to suffer anymore. When YOU decide to feel good, not bad. When YOU decide to use your life to enjoy life and all it has to offer you.

Think about it. The next time you find yourself in a not-so-feeling-good situation, step back. Consciously stop judging yourself and others. Pause. Look at what is going on, objectively, like you are watching a movie of somebody else's life. Invariably, you will notice someone who is unhappily or unknowingly participating in, or fueling, discontent with their words. When you can detach from reacting and come from a place of higher understanding -- looking in, so to speak -- you will see quite clearly a deeper understanding meant for you. Call it "taking the high road" or "loving indifference." That "something" can be as simple as forgiveness or patience or being kind. It might be just another opportunity to practice a deeply satisfying feeling of inner calm amidst chaos. It might be a clearer sense of how to respond and be present, rather than reacting and causing greater harm. No matter what lesson awaits you, you will discover a deepening awareness of your own strengths, preferences, likes and dislikes, passion, and wisdom. You will identify more with who you truly want to be in this lifetime.

Some people say, "But what if they are wrong and I am right?" Our answer is, there is no right or wrong. The only meaning anything ever has is that which you give it, and meanings change. Allow others to be right. It is a small price to pay for a healthy mental outlook, inner peace, and calm. It is another way of "letting go." Never mind how others are vibrating. Your only concern should be how to hold the vibration that feels good to you.

How do you do this? How do we let go of past mistakes and blunders? Gratitude. Gratitude that you do not feel their pain. Gratitude that you know more about how life works. Gratitude that they are teaching you more about who you want to be. Be grateful, because the best part of gratitude is once you find it, there's nothing left to hold on to. Proverbial "baggage" vaporizes into thin air. You know why?

You can't be grateful and angry at the same time.

You can't be grateful and sad at the same time.

You can't be grateful and jealous at the same time.

You can't be grateful and lonely at the same time.

And you can't be grateful and hurt at the same time.

> Allow yourself to love yourself. Look around you. Let go of all the baggage you have carried for years -- it no longer exists.
> Be present, and find your inner strength. Know that every experience that brought you pain made you who you are today. Without it, you would not be YOU. Find gratitude for all that life has caused you to become.
> Let it go. Free your mind.

You can only be grateful. Finding gratitude is the fastest way to bring yourself into harmony with the greater part of you: your inner self, your Inner Guidance, inner peace, and calm. This is how we begin to truly tap into the powerful source that lives within each and every one of us. We all have this power, so how can we tap into it all the time? By changing the way we speak to ourselves and about ourselves to others. We can change the way we think, which changes the way we perceive our lives. Your mind is the passage to your soul. Learn to communicate with your "self" in a loving, kind, and compassionate way and you will open the door to the power that is within you – the power that is within all of us.

The only thing that you can ever change is you. Make it a priority to be in alignment with YOU, the greater part of you, and everything in your life will resonate with your true authentic self. We do not have to change others to get what we want. The only thing that we have to change is what we want to see. Use your conversations to practice verbalizing what you want to see. Shift your conversations, and your thoughts will follow. Start talking about only what you want, never what you don't want, and you will begin to vibrate in a way that feels good to YOU.

Be grateful. When your conversations are full of, "I am so incredibly grateful for each day that I am given, I am grateful for the roof over my head, the clothes that I wear, the food I eat, the heat that keeps me warm on long winter nights, the sun that wakes me in the morning, my family and friends, my job that provides the means to live comfortably," you are living a deeply satisfying life. Gratitude begets gratitude. Being grateful feels like abundance. Being grateful is how you feel an abundant life.

Be in harmony with who you are inside, right here, right now. Keep up with all that life is causing you to become. Listen in on every conversation. Each one tells you immediately what vibration you are offering and you will immediately know exactly what you are allowing to flow your way. What you talk about, you think about and what you think about, you get back, every single time.

CHAPTER SEVEN
BE THE POWERFUL BEING YOU ARE MEANT TO BE

*Your life is a story. My life is a story. Humanity's existence is a story.
What is the story of your life? Is it a string of random events? Is it
boring? Is it compelling? Is it shallow? Is it deep? What will be the
next act in your story? The next scene? The next message? What
story are your beliefs creating and how do you feel as it unfolds? You
are the creator, director and star of your life and story.*

CHANGE YOUR CONVERSATION IS ABOUT changing the way you
talk to yourself and others around you so that you are connecting
with the true authentic source of all sources that lives within each and
every one of us. It's about understanding just how powerful you are
and learning how to use that power to create a life that feels like the
happiness, love, and joy that we are all looking for.

The happiness we seek is within ourselves. Being happy is nothing
more than deciding to take your power back, owning it, respecting
it, embracing it, and taking total responsibility for the world that you
are creating.

To be happy is to trust yourself, to be comfortable with yourself
and align yourself with honesty and integrity. When you allow your-
self to love and accept your body and the pleasure stored within it,
you are allowing yourself to connect with the power within you …
YOU! Learn to harness your strengths and be the powerful being you
are meant to be!

Happiness is not dependent on whether we have problems any more than it is dependent on material wealth. Happiness is a reflection of your beliefs about yourself and the world around you. Challenge your beliefs, one by one. Look at them from a different point of view. Does this belief make me happy? If your belief is solid, it will stand up under this scrutiny. If not, let it go and be happy.

Learn to be happy where you are, because no matter where you go, there you are. So many times we think we have to get somewhere in order for our lives to be better, to be perfect, to be happy, to be all we want it to be. It all begins right here, right now. If you can't be happy with who you are where you are now, how will you be happy further down the road? Find your peace from within; find your true happiness.

You are the seeker. You are entitled to your own beliefs, but you are also accountable for your own morality and enlightenment. Your path is your own, but you must walk side by side with others with compassion. The only thing that is required is fearlessness: fearlessness in your examination of life and death, willingness to continually grow, and openness to the possibility that all your joys and sorrow have meaning.

We are conditioned to not look at the cause of our pain and suffering, instead we use labels: I have a chemical imbalance, I'm an alcoholic, I'm addicted, I'm obsessive-compulsive, I'm not worthy. It all boils down to our running away from the things that cause pain in our lives. Until we look at our pain, it will never go away. To find true happiness we have to align our minds, hearts, and souls. We have to be courageous enough to be who we are.

Nobody said it would be easy to look pain in the eye, but it seems to us much harder to carry a burden around for years rather than to hit it straight on, deal with it, and get on with it. Little by little, start looking in the slightest of ways at those painful memories, and put them to rest; be grateful for all that they have given you, and start living life!

Everything you have ever done has increased your love and understanding of yourself and others, even when you didn't know it. Just look at the lives you have touched. Just look at you. Learn to love yourself just the way you are. Most of us think of ourselves as not being good enough or not having enough, or not being a good enough parent or spouse. Relax. You are doing the very best that you can do. When you realize that there is a better way or that you can do better, you will, just as you have always done. You are already halfway there.

> In order to see the change we wish to see, we have to be the change we wish to see. If you want others to stop judging, you stop judging. If you want others to be more kind, you be more kind. If you want others to stop talking about you, you stop talking about others. It always begins and ends with you.

Learn to love yourself and all that you have become. Without every experience that you have had thus far, you would not be the person you are today. Look at all of your experiences as a chance to grow. When you can be thankful for these experiences, you can then love them and then love yourself. As Frank Allen observes in *Chaos Theory*, "The most important thing about love is that we choose to give it and we choose to receive it, making it the least random act in the entire universe."

Approach your life with an open mind, a creative mind, a loving mind. Be gentle with yourself. Trust that you will continue to lay down difficulties like old clothes that no longer fit or that you choose not to wear. Realize that it is you who is designing experiences for your greatest need and growth. Do not be afraid of moving forward; it is what you are meant to do.

When we say and feel that we are stuck in a situation or have no options, understand that it is your thinking that has gotten you there. You are not stuck without options available to you; there are always options and opportunities. It is only that you are not opening yourself up to the many opportunities that are around you. Stop limiting your thoughts and watch the world open up.

When you are in a state of confusion and recognize it as such, congratulate yourself. You are scrambling up old behavior patterns and beliefs so that you can bring better alignment to your life. Do not feel you are going nowhere. This is rich breeding ground for change as long as you do not stay there. You will not stay there when you honor, surrender, and acknowledge that you are working on something … change.

In order for change to happen, you have to want change. You have to be asking for change. Asking for change is opening yourself to experience something more. Asking for change is allowing your brain to open up to new possibilities; it's prompting the brain to start looking for new information. Change happens only when we begin looking and wanting to see something different -- only then can the brain see it! Life is forever changing. Everything around you changes, grows, and evolves; it is our job to go with the change, not resist it. So many times we find ourselves wanting to hold on to the past. We want to keep things the same. We don't want to change. Nothing ever stays the same -- we are meant to continually evolve and grow. Every event or circumstance, person, place, or thing that you have experienced has been given to you for you to learn from and evolve with. These contrasts, both good and bad, are your opportunities to dig deep and find meaning, redefine once again who you truly are, and jump. Catapult yourself to the next level of life. Use the contrasts as springboards that launch you one step closer to where you truly want to be.

Change or contrast is nothing more than life offering you limitless possibilities to choose a better path. This is where the fun begins. Don't let yourself get caught up in not letting go or being afraid of what is to come. Know that you are your own creator, trust in yourself, believe in yourself -- and when an opportunity presents itself ... MOVE!

As adults, we forget that life is supposed to be fun. We forget how to let ourselves go, get out of the way, and allow ourselves to dream. Everything around you at one point was nothing but a dream. When we stop thinking and start dreaming, start believing in our dreams, start believing in ourselves and following our waves of desire, we remember how fun this journey can be.

We wish there were words to tell you how beautiful life really is, how safe you always are, and of the love that surrounds you ... how powerful you are, how much you can have, and of the joy that awaits ... of the magic, the perfection, and the infinite possibilities. Give your brain permission to have these things, and they will become your things. Set your imagination free!

If we always look at "what is," we continue to get more of "what is." Allowing ourselves to dream big allows us to move beyond what stares us in the face, gives us hope, expansion, and inspiration. Anything is possible if you believe ... so start believing in yourself!

> If we believe that nothing happens to us that does not belong to us, we take greater responsibility for our actions and absolutely enjoy greater control of our lives.
>
> ༄

When you feel yourself spinning your wheels, can't find an answer, or are not sure what direction to go, understand that at that moment, you're trying to push your way to the answer. Instead, disengage, relax, let that thought completely go, center yourself, and get quiet. Look at the end result of where you want to be, and let go. Don't give any other thought a second thought. When you least expect it, BOOM, there it is! It's just that simple!

Your job is to look for it. Look for what you want because you'll know it when you feel it. If you question the path you are on, just ask yourself, how do I feel? How do *I* feel? Always choose the path that feels good to you.

This is how you consult the greater part of you and let your feelings guide you. Does this thought that I'm thinking right now bring me a sense of relief? Does this thought that I'm thinking right now feel like the expanded part of me that I want to manifest? This comes down to the law of attraction. What you choose to give your attention to will be the energy or vibration that you are offering to the universe. Just know what energy you are offering and ask yourself, do you want that same energy to come back to you? Because that which you put out is what you will get back.

Whatever road you choose to take (and there are endless possibilities), take your time and go down every single one of them in your mind, and when you do, allow yourself to feel them. Does that one make me angry? Does that one make me upset? Does that one make me feel good? Does that one make me happy? Does that one make me feel like I'm doing the right thing? Above all else, how do I feel? The one that feels like a sense of relief ... that's the one. That's the one you're looking for. You're looking for the burning sensation in the core of your being. Like when you get excited about a new opportunity for a higher position in the company, or just found out that you got accepted into the college of your choice, or just met the partner of your dreams. That feeling of inspiration, an undeniable calling toward, is the feeling of the greater part of you telling you this is the way you want to go. You are seeing that which you are thinking about through the eyes of your inner guidance. You are connecting to and harnessing your power.

Here's the catch: most of us can connect and roll with the feeling of inspiration and start out on a journey of discovery, and then what happens? Your mind starts playing tricks on you. You start having conversations that sound like: "Who do I think I am? How can I possibly pull that off? Do I really think I'm capable of doing that?" Or, we hear others around us telling us the odds that are stacked against us or telling us that they would never step out on a limb like that. Immediately we allow ourselves to fall right back into the same old habitual pattern of thinking, without even recognizing it. This is where you have to be listening in on the conversations you are having with you. You have to take control and tell the brain where you want it to go. You have to be continually giving your mind new information to move it in the direction you want to go. Where the brain goes, the body follows.

The next thing that happens is we think we have to plan out every step along the way and we have to figure out how in the world we are going to make things happen. It's NEVER about the how. When we begin trying to figure out the how, we begin measuring where we are in comparison to where we want to be, which does nothing more than hold your vibration where you are. Keep your eye on the end result – what you want – and have faith and trust that the universe will respond as it always has to line up everything that you will need to get you where you want to go.

Here's an example: If you are wanting a relationship, it's not who, it's what. What kind of person am I looking for? What role do I want this person to play in my life? What are the most important qualities to me? What would bring me the most joy? What values and morals resonate with my own? Become very clear, down to the smallest of details of what would bring you happiness. Allow yourself to imagine your perfect match to the point that you can see them, smell them, touch them, hear them in your mind -- and when you can FEEL that … LET IT GO.

Your job is to simply be present, relaxed, and looking for any and every opportunity - however subtle or great - that will lead you one step closer to where you want to be. The more you learn to lean downstream, to go with the flow, the faster the flow becomes. The more opportunities begin to present themselves and the faster you get to where you want to be. And the more opportunities that present themselves, the more gratitude you feel; and the more gratitude you feel, the greater the vibration you hold and the more you receive. And so we begin creating a new state of being.

> When you are feeling a little unsure, when you need a little confidence, sometimes all you need to do is remind yourself this is my dream and everybody I see, is in it.
>
> ∽∾

Start looking for the feeling of what you are wanting to experience, and you will begin to see more and more opportunities to choose that feeling. You will begin to meet others who reflect back to you the feeling that you are now intentionally creating. The universe will begin to respond to the new vibration you are holding yourself to, and your world will start shifting right in front of your eyes.

Ask and it is given: every single time, no exceptions. Everything that you need to move your life in the direction that you want to go is right within reach. Everything that you need to make your dreams come true is hovering around you, waiting to be seen. It's your job to be open, available, and ready to receive all that you have been asking for. When you see it, you will know it; when you know it, act on it. Every time you practice feeling what it is you are wanting, you give your brain permission to see something new.

When you see an opportunity, which is simply something your brain has never seen before, it is your job to take that opportunity and run with it. When you feel that burning desire within yourself, act on it. Don't second-guess yourself or talk yourself out of something you truly want. Don't ask others around you what they think; it doesn't matter what someone else thinks. All that matters is that you connect with that inner passion and ride the wave of desire!

Your outside always reflects your inside. When we learn to follow our waves of desire and learn to use our feelings as our guidance system to a better-feeling life, our outside world will reflect the happiness that we feel inside.

It's amazing how everything begins to fall right into place when we allow ourselves to become incredibly clear about how we want to feel on every level of our lives, without allowing the input or expectations of others to get in the way. If we simply tune in, relax, create, and then lie back and allow ourselves to receive what we are creating, life becomes magical, expansive, and exciting!

When you start to understand the law of attraction and that everything you put out you get back, amazing things start to happen. All of a sudden all of the things that you have been asking for start appearing in the strangest of places and the greatest of times. Our job is to allow ourselves to have what we so desperately have been asking for. All of us ask … but do you allow?

Allowing yourself to have all that life has caused you to ask for is the key to receiving. Most give up on their hopes and dreams too early along the path. If we come to terms with faith and trusting

that everything is laid out in front of us each step of the way just as it needs to be, then we can let go of our fears, we begin to see the gifts already here waiting to be seen.

Sometimes we forget that we can create whatever we want. When we align ourselves with our own light, we cannot help the unfolding of the greatest fulfillment of our being. It is our job to create balance within our lives and allow the joy that balance brings to open doorways where we now see walls. Keep the self centered and doorways will open through your relaxing, and waiting, to see what you are creating. You have to be looking for what you say you want. You have to be ready for a greater experience when you see it.

This is your dream, this is your world. Create it the way you want it to be. If this is not what you want in your life, simply look around, turn your direction, shift yourself, and look at what is sitting right next to you. What do you want that to be? Start putting your energy where you want it. Be intentional about it. This is where you get to start fine-tuning. Step back and look. Look at where you are directing your energy. Is this the energy you want coming back to you? Is this the wave you want to ride?

When you get out of the way and start allowing yourself to be who you really are, despite the good opinions of others, connect with the core of your being and know that, "This is who I really am and this is what I really want," AMAZING things start to happen all around you. Everything you have dreamed of begins to line itself up right before your very eyes.

Letting go of what the expectations and opinions of others are, or what others think you should do, allows us to clear our minds and truly spend time with ourselves. What works for others is not necessarily what works for you. Allowing yourself to stand on your own and soar through the sky, being everything and anything you choose, is the most freeing, expansive, joyous, and inspiring feeling one could ever experience!

You are only as strong, independent, courageous, or amazing as you allow yourself to be. The only thing stopping you or standing in your way is YOU. When you can stop judging yourself, beating yourself up, or sizing yourself to others or for others, you free yourself to see just who you really are and how you truly have the capability to be all you yearn to become. Your job is to dream big, let it go, and have faith. Trust yourself that when an opportunity arises to move your dreams one step closer to reality, you will know it and MOVE ... physically and mentally MOVE!

It all comes down to energy. Where can you put your energy that is going to best serve you? It doesn't matter who, what, where, why, or how ... it's the end result. Where do you want to be? And that makes it so simple. Get past what's staring you in the face and look at what is beyond. Move your energy somewhere else and that which you do not want will fade away while being replaced by that which you are asking for.

Through thinking, feeling, doing, dreaming, speaking, intending, wishing, and being you emit energy all the time. What are you contributing to? Are you contributing to the energy of joy or despair? Are you clear about what you want and how you want to feel? Do you know you can create any version of life you desire? Learn to notice what you are thinking about and focus your thoughts -- this is how dreams come true.

If you want a life that you love, start making it a life that you love. Start looking at where you're putting your energy with your thoughts because that's where it all starts.

When you notice how *Change Your Conversation* moves your life, turn around and share this new way of looking at things with family and friends. Practice a better-feeling conversation together. Our goal is to touch a million lives and have that million turn around and touch a million more. You are part of this karmic wave of changing conversations we are creating together. Now turn around and help others to know.

Peace, love, and happiness,

~ Malinda and Lani

Life can be as amazing as you allow it to be. We all have our bumps in the road, mountains to climb, and fears to face. The question is, do you stand at the foot of the mountain too afraid to even try -- or do you dig deep, give it everything you've got, and conquer? The higher the mountain, the greater the fear, the greater the growth. Trust in yourself. Believe in yourself. Free yourself.

CHAPTER EIGHT
THINK ABOUT IT

1. Where attention goes, energy flows.

   What you talk about, you think about; and what you think about, you bring about, every single time.

2. Your brain is a piece of equipment.

   Practice the life you want. Practice the relationships you want. Practice loving yourself. Do this with every thought, act, and intent. It is OK to feel like you are just going through the motions or mouthing the words. That's the practice part. It is intent your mind pays attention to. The universe is nothing more than a big copying machine. You get back what you feel inside. That's the intent part. Practice the life you want.

3. We are walking, talking, energy beings.

   The only thing standing between you and the life of your dreams is you.

4. What are you giving your attention to?

   Are you carrying around junk from five, ten, or even twenty

years ago? Stop and ask yourself why. Those experiences no longer exist. If we hold ourselves in the past, then how can we enjoy the present? How can we experience more of what we want? Take a step back from experiences that you are holding on to, find the lesson with them, and allow yourself to let them go. Free yourself from junk and get on with life.

5. Every thought has a feeling.

   It takes will and determination to take control of your thoughts. You have to first decide if you care enough about YOU to want to feel good. Then you have to observe your thoughts and non-judgmentally ask yourself, "Is this what I really want? Is this where I really want to be?" Then you have to dig deep and find a better-feeling thought to replace the old thought with. Once you have found it, hold on to it. Allow yourself to feel empowered all over again.

6. Inner Guidance is the part of you that never changes.

   As you prepare for each day, look in the mirror at the beautiful being staring back at you. Allow yourself to love yourself. Allow yourself to connect with that part of you that never changes, the part of you that has always felt the same, the part of you that still feels young, vibrant, excited, and worry-free. Allow yourself to remember who you really are.

7. What do you choose?

   As we walk through life we are all looking for the same thing: to be happy. When we stop looking "out there" for something or someone to make us happy, and start taking responsibility for our own happiness, it is then that we find it. We find it inside ourselves by choosing to love every bit of who we are and what we are always becoming.

8. What is the power of conversation?

Practice talking to yourself about what you want. Practice thinking about what you want. Practice saying what you want. Practice saying what you want with confidence, and knowing, and feeling. Because if you can't talk about what you want, you don't know what you want. And, if you can't see what you want, you'll never have what you want. You have to see it and feel it down to the minutest detail to have it.

9. We all have a story.

No one escapes experience. It is all around you. The fundamental truth about experience is that most cannot be changed; they must be transcended.

10. Turn your conversation around.

You are the writer of the script of your life and everyone in it is playing the part you have assigned to them.

11. Be the powerful creator you are meant to be.

As adults, we forget that life is supposed to be fun. We forget how to let ourselves go, get out of the way, and allow ourselves to dream. Everything around you at one point was nothing but a dream. When we stop thinking about "what is" and start dreaming and believing in "what could be," we will remember how fun this journey can be.

12. How do I attract a healthy relationship?

Most of us try to run away from ourselves and our feelings. Feelings need to be felt and accepting responsibility for how you feel not only puts you in touch with your beliefs, you will also be operating from a stance of empowerment. Listen to what the greater part of you is telling you. Allow your feelings to guide you. It is never the person, it is always the feeling of how you want the relationship to feel.

13. You are in total control.

The beauty of life is that there is always a choice. When we want something, choose to go for it and then realize, Well, maybe I don't want this … we get to choose again. There is never a reason to feel stuck or trapped in a situation. We are always choosing. Listen to yourself, your inner guidance, and you will always find yourself in control of where you are and what you are choosing to be.

14. Put the law of attraction to work for you.

Whether you are in a relationship or not, whether you have a family or not, you are on this journey alone. So many times we put ourselves in a bad relationship or make not-so-great choices because we are afraid of being alone. You are alone. You are the only one walking around in your life. You are the only one who can see your path. You are the only one who can make choices for your life. You are the only one who knows what is best for you.

15. Listen to your Inner Guidance.

As life comes your way, take the time to pause and feel the possibilities that exist around you. If you go with the first thing that comes along and do not consult the greater part of you, how you feel, you are shooting in the dark. Take control of your life and where you are going by stepping back and allowing yourself to see possibilities in every experience. Slow down and choose what feels best for you.

16. Moving your thoughts.

Why do we make things more complicated than they need to be? Why do we try to take on other people's experiences? When we understand that their deal is not our deal, any more than our deal is their deal, we begin to be kind, and to approach the lives created by others with loving indifference, or "Honey, I love you but I cannot help you." This means we can help guide them back to their power without giving away any of our power at the same time.

17. How do I stop making the same mistakes?

Everything starts with you. If you are wanting a relationship or to change a relationship that you are in, you have to have the relationship you want with yourself first before you can ever have it with anyone else. If you are wanting more respect from your peers, you have to respect yourself first. If you want your spouse to be more open, you must be more open. If you want others to be more kind, you be more kind. Everything in your life is a reflection of you.

18. How you think determines how you feel.

One of the biggest mistakes we make is thinking we can change somebody to be more of what we need them to be. When we try to make someone change to make us feel better, we give away our gift of personal growth, and it does not feel good. We say, "You grow for me, you do it," when we could just do it ourselves and feel our power again.

19. Purify yourself every night.

Some people are so concerned with "doing good" that they never find love for themselves and end up being unable to help others. The most unselfish people know themselves so well that they no longer feel a need to control others, manipulate, sulk, whine, or be depressed or angry in any way to get what they want. They radiate freedom and fearlessness through self-knowledge and self-love, and inspire others to give themselves permission to feel the same.

20. This is a commitment to you.

In order to change your experience you must change your

beliefs. You must first believe it is possible to create a healthy body, a healthy bank account, and healthy relationships. Then you must begin crafting the reality you want – first, by ceasing to participate in limiting activities, then by creating a clear detailed mental image of your desired outcome. You must expect results or there will be none.

21. Change Your Conversation.

Everything starts with a thought, and that thought turns into a conversation that we have with ourselves, and that internal conversation turns into the conversations we have with others. To create a better-feeling life, you have to begin paying attention to the thoughts and conversations you participate in with yourself and others. Your world is reflected in your words. Where the mind goes, the body follows. Be the powerful creator you are -- because you are.

CHAPTER NINE
WHO TAUGHT US

1. **His Holiness the Dalai Lama on *How to See Yourself as You Really Are*:** "Exist without misconception."

2. **Dr. Wayne Dyer on *The Power of Intention*:** "You'll see it when you believe it."

3. **Deepak Chopra on *The New Physics of Healing*:** "To think is to practice brain chemistry."

4. **Debbie Ford:** "Many of us are frightened to look within ourselves, and fear has us put up walls so thick we no longer remember who we really are. By choosing not to allow parts of ourselves to exist, we are forced to expend huge amounts of psychic energy to keep them beneath the surface."

5. **Barbara de Angelis on *How Did I Get Here?*** "Beyond your challenges, beyond your successes, beyond the events with which life has molded your spirit, there is a placeless place within you. It is a place of peace. It is a place of freedom. It is the place where the Self you have been seeking resides."

6. **Pema Chondron on *Start Where You Are:*** "If someone instructed you to catch the beginning, middle, and end of every thought, you'd find they don't seem to have a beginning, middle, and end. They definitely are there. You're talking to yourself, you're creating your whole identity, your whole world, your whole sense of problem, your whole sense of contentment, with this continual stream of thought. But if you really try to find thoughts, they are always changing."

7. **Science Daily on Language:** "This study suggests that language is much more than a medium for expressing thoughts and feelings. Our work hints that language creates and shapes our thoughts and feelings as well." http://www.sciencedaily.com/releases/2010/11/101103111206.htm

8. **Cameron Day on *Multi-dimensional Energy Biology*:** "Quantum physics and ancient spiritual teachings agree that our experience of reality is determined by our beliefs and thought patterns. Neuroplasticity continually reinforces the patterns of thought that we are comfortable with, causing information that runs counter to one's beliefs to be ignored, while information that supports those beliefs is embraced. In order to understand more deeply how our belief systems affect our experience of reality, we need to understand the basic mechanics by which we attract 'higher dimensional' energy that matches our frequency." http://www.ascensionhelp.com/multi-dimensional-cell-biology.php

9. **Sheena Iyenger on *The Art of Choosing*:** "The value of choice depends on our ability to see differences between options." http://www.ted.com/talks/lang/eng/sheena_iyengar_on_the_art_of_choosing.html

10. **Fred Alan Wolf on *What's Luck Got to Do With It?*** "Because we don't typically pay attention to ourselves in the perception process, our immediate experience usually will not appear to show how our act of perception changed anything. However, if we construct a careful history of our perceptions, it will often show us that our way of perceiving did indeed change the course of our personal history." The Dream Manifesto, http://www.dreammanifesto.com/whats-luck.html

11. **Michael Talbot on *The Amazing Holographic Universe:*** "In 1982 a remarkable event took place. At the University of Paris, a research team led by physicist Alain Aspect performed what may turn out to be one of the most important experiments of the 20th century. You did not hear about it on the evening news. In fact, unless you are in the habit of reading scientific journals you probably have never even heard Aspect's name, though there are some who believe his discovery may change the face of science. *Aspect and his team discovered that under certain circumstances subatomic particles such as electrons are able to instantaneously communicate with each other regardless of the distance separating them. It doesn't matter whether they are 10 feet or 10 billion miles apart.*" The Dream Manifesto, http://www.dreammanifesto.com/amazing-holographic-universe.html

12. **The Mystery of Consciousness:** http://homepage.mac. com/dbhill/mystery_of_consciousness.html

13. **Buddhist Teaching on Being Awake**: "When the Buddha started to wander around India shortly after his enlightenment, he encountered several men who recognized him to be a very extraordinary being. They asked him: 'Are you a god?' 'No,' he replied. 'Are you a reincarnation of a god?' 'No,' he replied. 'Are you a wizard, then?' 'No.' 'Well, are you a man?' 'No.' 'So what are you?' they asked, being very perplexed. Buddha simply replied: 'I am awake.' Buddha means 'the awakened one.' How to awaken is all he taught."

14. **Mother Teresa on Love:** "If we really want to love others, we must first begin to love one another in our own home. Love begins at home, and so from here – from our own home – love will spread to my neighbor, in the street I live, in the town I live, in the whole world."

15. **Barbara Marciniak on *The Path of Empowerment:*** "Everyone here on Earth is here to participate in and contribute to the mass awakening of humanity to the truth that your thoughts create your reality." ~ The Pleiadians

16. **Jack Kornfield on *A Path With Heart*:** "It is not necessary for you to evaluate the practices chosen by others. Remember, the practices themselves are only vehicles for you to develop awareness, loving-kindness, and compassion on the path toward freedom. That is all."

17. **Lynne McTaggert on Intention,** *Down the Rabbit Hole:* "Your intention is going to affect your world. Your thoughts, your very thoughts, affect your life. You have to think wisely, intentionally."

18. **Ramtha on Reality,** *Down the Rabbit Hole*: "How do I create my reality? You are the reality you are creating."

19. **Joe Dispenza, D.C. on** *Evolve Your Brain*: "To think inside the box is to cause our mind to fire in the most regular way in which we fire our own pattern of neural circuits, based on what we know and remember. To think outside the box, then, is to force the brain to fire synaptic patterns in different orders and arrangements to make a new level of mind, based on what we do not know."

20. **Barbara Marciniak on** *The Family of Light*: "How you think and communicate is how you know yourself and how you arrive at your beliefs about yourself. Clear communication is the essence of understanding." ~ The Pleiadians

21. **Neale Donald Walsch on** *Conversations with God, Book 3***:** "You don't have to do anything. It is all a question of what you are being."

22. **Elizabeth Lesser on** *The New American Spirituality:* "We could say that the history of human suffering is our inability to come to terms with spiritual hunger. Like one big cosmic joke, humans were born yearning for a home of tranquil abiding, yet without a map to get there. In every

age some people seem to know more than others about the way home. They have been called shamans, prophets and messiahs, monks and gurus, poets and philosophers, scientists and psychologists. They spend most of their time contemplating the way home and reporting their findings. Religions and big bang theories are attributed to their wisdom. Yet when all is said and done, each one of us is left abiding in the mystery, longing for the tranquility that is whispered about in the depths of our own hearts. Thus a critical step on the spiritual path, the one that we will take over and over, is to let ourselves experience spiritual hunger long enough and deep enough to follow it to its source."

23. **Neale Donald Walsch on *Questions and Answers on Conversations with God*:** "Every thought creates. What it creates is up to you."

24. **Zeitgeist the Movie, Zeitgeist: Addendum, and Zeitgeist: Moving Forward** http://www.zeitgeistmovie.com/

25. **Abraham through Esther Hicks**: "You are never satisfied. That's what life is, it's just this ongoing, never-ending vacation adventure, you see. You can't get it wrong and you never get it done – and we recommend that you have as much fun as you can along the way."

26. **Annie Shapiro on *The Tibetan Book of the Dead*:** "The Tibetan Book of the Dead is actually a manual for the living. It details the journey each soul must make after death

as reported back by meditators who used their lives to journey on other planes and bring back information about how reality is constructed."

27. **Mike Dooley on *Notes from the Universe:*** "For those who don't yet understand themselves, it's impossible that they might understand you. Impossible."

28. "Be kind, for everyone you meet is fighting a great battle." Philo of Alexandria, **www.gratefulness.org**

PROLOGUE

Practice.

ALSO BY *CHANGE YOUR CONVERSATION*

DVDs

Online Study

Seminars and Workshops

Audio Downloads

Free Daily Thoughts

One-On-One Coaching

www.changeyourconversation.com

"Before there was *Change Your Conversation,* the book, there was just my really great friend, Lani, having numerous dialogues with me regarding some of the obstacles life seems to throw our way. What I thought was just a 'friend helping a friend' was actually Lani guiding me to change my conversations with myself.

"It is logical:
'Go with the feeling.'

"It has direction and purpose:
'Find the vibration and hold it.'

"It just makes sense:
'Be grateful ... you had that experience to show you what you do want.'

"How utterly empowering to turn your blame away from everything else and find a way to change your perspective for the positive!
'Turn it around,' she would say.
What a significantly more pleasant way to live when you have the power of understanding yourself!

"Now, Lani and Malinda are giving everyone the same tremendous opportunity to change their conversation and change their lives. Do you feel it yet? Listen to your feeling and not your thinking.

This book truly gives off a vibration that feels good.

"Go ahead. *Change Your Conversation, Change Your Life.*

It really works."

Mary Morton
Air Traffic Controller
Leesburg, Virginia
2011

Photograph of authors by: Erin Taylor

CPSIA information can be obtained at www.ICGtesting.com
Printed in the USA
269618BV00003B/53/P